✔ KU-686-735

THRIVING IN YOUR WORK

How to be Motivated and
Do Well in Challenging Times

Peter Shaw

LIS - LIBRARY

Date	Fund
04/09/14	

Order No.	
DONATION ·	

University of Chester

mc **Marshall Cavendish**
Business

Copyright © 2012 Peter Shaw

Cover design by Opalworks Pte Ltd

Published in 2012 by Marshall Cavendish Business
An imprint of Marshall Cavendish International

PO Box 65829
London EC1P 1NY
United Kingdom
info@marshallcavendish.co.uk
and

1 New Industrial Road, Singapore 536196
genrefsales@marshallcavendish.com
www.marshallcavendish.com/genref

Other Marshall Cavendish offices: Marshall Cavendish International (Asia) Private Limited, 1 New Industrial Road, Singapore 536196 • Marshall Cavendish Corporation, 99 White Plains Road, Tarrytown, NY 10591 • Marshall Cavendish International (Thailand) Co Ltd. 253 Asoke, 12th Flr, Sukhumvit 21 Road, Klongtoey Nua, Wattana, Bangkok 10110, Thailand • Marshall Cavendish (Malaysia) Sdn Bhd, Times Subang, Lot 46, Subang Hi-Tech Industrial Park, Batu Tiga, 40000 Shah Alam, Selangor Darul Ehsan, Malaysia

Marshall Cavendish is a trademark of Times Publishing Limited

The right of Peter Shaw to be identified as the author of this work has been asserted by him in accordance with the Copyright, Designs and Patents Act 1988.

All rights reserved

No part of this publication may be reproduced, stored in a retrieval system or transmitted, in any form or by any means, electronic, mechanical, photocopying, recording, or otherwise, without the prior permission of the copyright owner. Requests for permission should be addressed to the publisher.

The author and publisher have used their best efforts in preparing this book and disclaim liability arising directly and indirectly from the use and application of this book.

All reasonable efforts have been made to obtain necessary copyright permissions. Any omissions or errors are unintentional and will, if brought to the attention of the publisher, be corrected in future printings.

A CIP record for this book is available from the British Library

ISBN 978 981 4346 50 4

Printed and bound in Great Britain by
CPI Group (UK), Croydon, CR0 4YY

Marshall Cavendish publishes an exciting range of books on business, management and self-development.

If you would like to:

- Find out more about our titles
- Take advantage of our special offers
- Sign up to our e-newsletter

Please visit our special website at: www.business-bookshop.co.uk

Dedicated to David Normington
who encouraged me to move into a second
career supporting and challenging leaders
so they can thrive in their work.

CONTENTS

FOREWORD

Thriving in your work and enabling others to thrive is crucial for success. Peter's approach captures the essential elements of this principle with his focus on clarity of outcome and impact, his emphasis on working as a team, developing new skills and approaches, and using time and energy well. Each section is short, clear and impactful.

At Grontmij we have a heritage of nearly a century of design and engineering consultancy based on geographical markets mainly in the Netherlands. Because of increased internationalisation and growing competition, I was convinced of the tremendous opportunities which would result from shifting our strategic focus from individual countries to market sectors across Europe.

We have now grown to a firm of 11,000 employees across Europe and beyond. We are fostering a truly European business pushing best practices and innovations across borders, attracting top quality professional engineers and new customers. We have integrated people from many cultures within one company who are addressing and overcoming challenges ranging from language barriers, different cultural backgrounds, different systems and reporting formats.

For Grontmij, transformational change has involved understanding what enables individuals to thrive at work when significant change is necessary within the organisation. We have sought to implement the new business approach and a European Grontmij culture in a positive way, without losing the strength of our inherited values and capabilities.

In several sessions for the top 50 leaders of Grontmij, Peter has helped us to "slice the elephant" into manageable pieces so that we have been agile in addressing daily business challenges, while ensuring that the overall long-term vision provides a consistent and inspirational context and approach. Peter has made us think in new ways and bring renewed energy in taking action forward, drawing on his wide international experience. It has given me joy and pleasure to see how much leadership teams can achieve through making a step a week together!

In *Thriving in Your Work*, Peter guides readers step-by-step in recognising the contribution they can make as a leader or manager in handling the changing reality in daily business, and in driving strategic change by inspiring and equipping others for a better future. Allowing yourself to reflect on each of the 52 themes in the book will bring new insights and joy both for you and for leadership teams. So much can be achieved just from making a step forward every week. This book will equip you to handle change well and thrive in everything that you do.

Sylvo Thijsen
Chief Executive, Grontmij NV
De Bilt, The Netherlands

INTRODUCTION

You are surviving in your work. Often you enjoy it, but at times you feel under a lot of pressure. Sometimes your work is rewarding and on other occasions, relentless.

You want to thrive in your work, but it is not always such a straightforward matter. You are reluctant to commit the time to read a management book from cover to cover, but you want the stimulus to help you do your work more effectively.

If you want to stretch your thinking and understand how you can thrive at work, this book is for you. It contains 52 short chapters looking at different aspects of thriving at work. Each chapter will share a story with you, set you thinking and pose questions for reflection.

The chapters are grouped under 12 main themes which provide food for thought over a period of one year, with the 52 chapters providing a point for reflection each week. The intention is to cover issues you face at work in an unorthodox way and give you a new angle to tackle them. Through reading this book, you will develop the ability to forget the irrelevant, see round corners, lay still and acknowledge when you are wrong. You will learn to use your energy more effectively and know when to trust your internal barometer, pound the pavements, have a "knees-up" and be able to see the brick wall coming.

I hope my book will provide a stimulus for thought and action by individuals, teams and groups in a range of sectors and countries. Do allow yourself to either work through the chapters sequentially over a period, or dip into whichever chapter relates to your particular circumstances. Be ready to mull over different ideas and approaches as you reflect on how best to thrive in your work.

My royalties from the book are going to the charity 'Feed the Minds', which funds a wide range of innovative education and literacy projects worldwide that aim to reduce poverty and build stronger communities.

Peter Shaw
Godalming
England

WHAT IS IT ALL FOR?

Fundamental to thriving in our work are a sense of purpose, clear reasons for endeavour, our sources of inspiration and those who accompany us on our journey.

When we are immersed in busy activities we may not often stand back to ask ourselves why we are where we are and why we work hard in the way we do. Time spent standing back can be valuable in enabling us to reflect on where we are going. The clearer we are about this, the more positive would be our approach to the future with our energy levels higher rather than lower.

This section looks in turn at 'where is the destination?', 'so why bother?', 'where does your inspiration come from?' and 'who are your companions along the way?'. Reasonable clarity about our answers to these questions will provide a good framework for working through the rest of the themes in the book.

01

WHERE IS THE DESTINATION?

Which mountain are you climbing?

On a couple of occasions I have walked across England from Arnside in Cumbria to Saltburn in North Yorkshire. The walk starts on the stone pier at Arnside and finishes at the end of the long iron pier at Saltburn. Throughout the walk, the image of Saltburn pier is a clear destination in my mind, especially when walking up the Pennines or the North York Moors.

When we have a clear destination, it gives us a reason for each step towards that destination. The destination might be reaching a particular level of responsibility, completing a project, a cadre of students receiving qualifications or getting jobs, a major commercial transaction agreed and delivered, or a budget outcome successfully reached. Sometimes it can help to visualise the destination so that the prospect of reaching that point can be an incentive that underpins all that we do.

When I walked across England, I reached an intermediate destination each evening. The distance each day was designed to be enjoyable, challenging and doable. Sometimes this destination was in view from a distance away. On other occasions, it was hidden in the mist, round the next corner or over the hill. I knew this destination was there even though I couldn't see it.

Perhaps the analogy here is that we need milestones towards our ultimate destination, while recognising that even these milestones may not be visible. But the fact that we know they are there helps keep up our focus and energy.

❖ Alan's story:

Alan wanted to open and run a restaurant. It had been his dream for years but when would it become a reality? Alan had the technical skills needed and a passion for setting up and running a restaurant. He could visualise what it would be like and the atmosphere within the restaurant. One day, Alan left his job and raised capital to get started. It was hard work with lots of disappointments along the way. He kept his resolve and retained in his mind's eye the restaurant he was going to create. Eventually, the restaurant was established, gained regular clientele and gradually became successful. The restaurant did not make Alan a fortune but it made him a living and gave him a life which he thoroughly enjoyed.

It is right to celebrate when we have reached a destination or delivered an outcome and it is justified to rest awhile, but our well-being may depend on then being clear about what our next destination is and how are we going to get there.

Sometimes external events dictate that our destination needs to change. We may be reluctant to do this because our course has been set. It can feel humiliating to change our destination but such flexibility is sometimes necessary and inevitable. For instance, we might get a new boss who wants different outcomes delivered; or the commercial realities may change so that what the market needs is a different focus. We may feel aggrieved that the requirements have changed, but the sooner we focus on the new destination, the better.

Sometimes we come to a realisation that the destination we are aiming for is the wrong one. This may result from an honest reassessment of our abilities and prospects. This process of readjustment may feel frustrating but where a destination is unattainable, our energy can be eroded and every step forward is much harder. Readjusting our destination to what is now attainable can both liberate us and lift our spirits.

Practical steps

Can you stand back and reflect on:

- What is the destination you would like to reach in 3–5 years' time?
- What are the next milestones towards reaching that ultimate destination?
- How realistic is that ultimate destination?
- How open are you to changing that destination?

As you reflect on the milestones over the next few weeks:

- Do these milestones fit into the overall picture of where you want to go?
- How flexible are you in considering the views of others about both the milestones and the ultimate destination?
- How helpful is it to have in your mind the type of ultimate destination you want to reach?

Clarity of destination can be helpful in giving a sense of direction. It can be unhelpful if it becomes too rigid and means that you've become blinkered. On a long distance walk you are forever balancing the image of the destination in your mind while enjoying all the vistas around you, each step of the way.

02

WHY BOTHER?

What is my motivation?

What gets you out of bed in the morning to go to work? Is it primarily because you need to earn money to put bread on the table? Is it because you are motivated by a particular type of activity? Is it because you see yourself as making a difference in a particular sphere?

Perhaps you are a teacher because you enjoy working with young people. Or you work in a hospital because caring for people and looking after their well-being is important to you. Perhaps you work in a commercial organisation because you believe that the country's economy needs to be strong so that public services can be paid for. Or you work for a charity because you believe that charities have a unique contribution to make in working with people who are not touched by the public or private sector. Perhaps our background, family heritage or faith perspective has given us the determination to succeed and want to make a difference; but at the same time, it is possible we can become too driven for our own good and become too blinkered or single-minded.

Might we be too bothered about too many details? Could it be that the best way forward is to stand back and observe how driven we are? Sometimes, we need to stand and stare and be amused by our own unrelenting sense of drive and ambition.

❖ **Geraldine's story:**

Coming from a family where no one had previously been to university, Geraldine wanted to study English and then to teach. She was determined to become the best teacher she could be; she loved her work and eventually became a head teacher. Friends admired her drive and respected the values that underpinned her work and her contribution to school life. When she retired she looked back on a fulfilling career and was grateful for the values she had inherited, but just sometimes she wonders if she could have stood back just a bit more. Perhaps she had been too determined to succeed and not widened her interests and friendships in a way that would have prepared her for retirement.

The ideal is to understand the causes of our motivation, yet not get too obsessed with them. If our motivation dampens, our effectiveness can diminish; but if our motivation goes into overdrive, then our actions can become counter productive and a source of irritation to others. Being "comfortable in yourself" is about living easily with yourself, knowing your passions and motivations, and sitting lightly to them. It is allowing ourselves to be motivated by our values and what matters to us, but not in an unrelenting way for 24 hours a day, seven days a week.

Practical steps

Some questions that might be worth revisiting are:

- What are my basic motivations in my work?
- Where do my values come from and do they continue to be important to me?
- When is my drive productive and when does it mean I become blinkered and less effective?
- When do I care too much and get over "bothered"?

As you reflect on the week ahead:

- When do you need to be focused and determined to deliver?
- When do you need to sit more lightly to a particular activity?
- How best are you comfortable with yourself so you bring both effective focus and the ability to stand back?

03 WHERE DOES YOUR INSPIRATION COME FROM?

Who lights your fire?

Who has been a source of inspiration for you? A friend shared stories about his father who had coped with the death of his wife and a painful illness. The main source of inspiration for my friend was the continuing influence of and friendship with his father who had shown such resilience through many years, who had "steel" in him which had kept him going through such personal struggles.

For another friend the main source of inspiration was a teacher who had inspired her to keep pushing the boundaries of her understanding. She changed from being a grumpy 15 year old to a motivated 18 year old, primarily because this teacher had believed in her and ignited a deep interest in the subject and filled her with a desire to go on to university and break into a new world.

For others the source of inspiration might be a mountaineer who achieved a remarkable climb; an adventurer who travelled a long distance in a small boat; a nun who gave up her worldly possessions to care and support others; or a politician who was prepared to be unpopular in order to campaign for a cause they felt passionate about.

Sometimes our inspiration might come from the achievements of historic figures. William Wilberforce wrote about being diligent in the business of life. He set his ambition on abolishing the slave trade which was not the best way of making himself popular. His legacy was to radically change accepted behaviour and to be an inspiration for many.

Our inspiration might come from our faith perspective. We want to serve others and make the world a better place. William Wilberforce felt called by his Christian convictions to seek the abolition of the slave trade. Our inspiration might consist of deeply held convictions that come from our faith understanding with an emphasis on new life and resurrection.

Our inspiration might also come from people in the community in which we live, such as those who have worked tirelessly in education or community activities to help grow in the next generation a desire to make lives more hopeful and less doomed to a cycle of low aspirations.

There will be those in the workplace who inspire us and those who depress us. Those who inspire us might do this because of their ability or attitude. It is likely that those who inspire us at work will be those who look positively to the future and are able to encourage and motivate those around them.

When we look for inspiration in the workplace, we do not seek hollow words. Inspiration that makes a difference links passion with performance, brings together a desire to make a difference with a depth of understanding and commitment. Inspiration that changes lives is never skin deep: it is always rooted in values and a deep understanding of the realities of what people are facing.

If we are inspired by one person or one cause, we can become one dimensional. Is there a mix of people who inspire us from different spheres? When people inspire us we often, even subconsciously, embrace some of their attitudes and approaches. When we are inspired by a number of people, we can blend from their characteristics that which best matches our personality and approach.

❖ Jack's story:

Jack was going through a tough time at work. The organisation was down-sizing and although he kept his job, there was no chance of promotion. The future looked dull. Jack reflected on what would be his sources of inspiration. He remembered his mother who, as a widow, had lived on a limited income and always kept cheerful. Jack thought of his youth leader who had cajoled Jack and his friends out of their lethargy and inspired them to complete the Duke of Edinburgh's Award for young people. Jack thought about a friend who was a marathon runner, whose single-mindedness in pacing himself to the finishing line inspired him.

Jack allowed himself to be inspired by others. This was no indulgence. He knew that in order to keep up his resolve he needed the inspiration of memories of people who had inspired him and conversations with friends who were a continuing source of inspiration to him.

Practical steps

As you look back:
- Who have been sources of inspiration to you?
- Who from history or from the wider world is a source of inspiration to you?
- Who in your workplace has inspired you?

As you look forward to the next few weeks:
- Who can you be a source of inspiration to?
- Whose example can you draw from as you work with others, so they too may be inspired by the illustrations you use?
- How willing are you to be inspired by an example of what someone else has contributed?

04 WHO ARE YOUR COMPANIONS ALONG THE WAY?

Who is committed to your success?

Many people do not miss their work when they retire, but they do miss their colleagues. Members of a project team who have worked well together may forget the nature of the project they were working on, but will have good memories of the team they were working in.

When I look back on my first career in government and my second career in developing leaders, I can recall vividly the people I most enjoyed working with. When you were working closely together to deliver a White Paper or a Parliamentary Bill on a particular time scale, there was a strong sense of co-operation and team work in generating the finished product on time. When a number of us set up our own businesses in the private sector in 2005, there was a powerful sense of working together to deliver a new business with character and energy.

A good companion is someone with whom you can share success and failure. With a good companion, you do not have to put a positive gloss on everything. Good conversation can embrace sharing success, working through difficult issues, devising new solutions and taking hard learning into a new sense of forward progress.

With a good companion you can express your frustrations and your hopes without fear of criticism. You can talk about difficult issues and not feel embarrassed. You can share when you feel indecisive and come out of the conversation encouraged rather than depressed.

Good companions at work can help us thrive. They can enable us to explore different possibilities and not feel a fear of criticism. They can enable us to dream dreams about the future without our feeling as if we are being arrogant and big-headed. We can think in radical new ways about how we can contribute, and feel that we are making progress rather than talking nonsense.

❖ Penny's story:

Penny was Managing Partner at a small accountancy firm. Looking back she remembered the encouragement she received from senior people when she started work at the practice. The most significant influence had come from a couple of colleagues. They had mentored each other and helped each other build up their practice. In regular conversations when someone was down, the others provided words of encouragement. There was a strong sense of the three of them being committed to each other's success. Gradually they went their different ways with the other two moving to different firms. Penny still meets up with her former colleagues and the quality of mutual support remains as strong as ever. They continue to be committed to each other's success and delighted in each other's company.

Being committed to each other's success can sound trite, but supportive relationships between colleagues that last longest are mutual. If they become one-sided for a long period they are likely, eventually, to die. Being committed to each other's success is about building a strong sense of mutuality even though the colleagues may be involved in very different spheres. It is about trying to create a win-win situation where both people feel they benefit from the companionship, while at the same time, being determined to support and encourage the other person.

For the last three years I have led a long distance walk for a dozen people during the first week of May. Through the course of the walk, you end up with a variety of different companions. Walking side-by-side you share stories, with friendships becoming ever stronger.

Thriving in your work is all the more likely if you have good companions along the way. In a fast changing work environment, it is necessary to build working relationships quickly. Creating a sense of companionship and shared endeavour early in a project can be so important to the project running smoothly.

But companionship is more than a means to an end. Companionship in a work context is to be enjoyed: it is not just about being productive. If we are in the same room as someone for eight hours a day, we can build a sense of either companionship or distance. We can choose our attitude and bring an openness and warmth towards generating a sense of companionship. Or we can bring a sense of distance which can limit what might otherwise be an enriching and enjoyable sharing and working together.

Creating good companions involves investing time and sharing of our own stories. Companionship to be effective has to be two-sided. It will mean showing our vulnerabilities and being willing to work and laugh together.

Practical steps

As you look back:

- Who have been your most important companions in your work?
- How has that companionship influenced your thinking and your attitude to work?

As you look forward:

- With whom are you committed to each other's success?
- How do you want to build more strongly that sense of companionship with colleagues?
- How can you treasure those people who have been good companions along the way and continue to be an important and creative influence upon you?

KEEP ALERT TO THE OUTCOMES

In this section I am using light as a metaphor to keep the focus on outcomes. Thriving in your work means continually coming back to what it is you are expected to deliver and how you keep a clear emphasis on the importance of delivery when life feels dull or black.

The themes in this section cover "who has got the torch", "recharging the batteries", "spotting the flicker" and "watch being blinded". One moment we can be clear about the outcomes we are seeking, while the next moment they seem vague or unattainable. It can sometimes be a case of "now you see it and now you don't". Part of thriving is in accepting that "this is the way it is", and that our steps to the outcomes aren't always as clear as we would wish.

05 WHO'S GOT THE TORCH?

If you have the torch do not be shy about using it

If you are in a dark place, the person with the torch has the prime responsibility to identify where you are and to see the possible next steps on the route. To be effective, the torch has to be held steadily and be focused on potential ways forward. If the torch is flashed round in a jerky way in lots of different directions, it is worse than useless as it blinds people and as a result their ability to see in the dark is diminished.

A torch has to be held steadily and used with purpose for it to be of value. A torch that is moved slowly up and down a particular direction can identify a route ahead and the obstacles on the way. Shining a light forward along the route ahead is akin to bringing an insight that clarifies the next steps. To throw light on an issue is to put it clearly into a wider perspective and to suggest reasons why a particular event or instance has happened.

In a team that is working well, the torch may well be passed round with each member taking it in turn to take the lead on a particular issue. For the torch bearer to lead the team effectively, the others have to trust in the torch bearer's judgement. Passing the torch round helps to reinforce that trust so it is built up and grown.

Sometimes we might want to pass the torch to a colleague because he or she has the experience and insight and can see next steps more clearly than others. Receiving the torch means accepting responsibility for the well-being and effectiveness of the whole group.

❖ Mel's story:

Mel was part of a project team which had gotten stuck. It felt as if they were in a cave and unable to find a way out. Whichever direction they went they would meet a rock wall. Gloom got hold of the team and they feared the project to provide a new product would have to be aborted. Mel, one of the younger members of the team, asked if he could have the opportunity to try a different approach. He asked people to use different assumptions to see if they could produce this product at a cost that was going to make it economically viable.

Mel was trying out thinking he had gleaned from elsewhere, coupled with ideas of his own. Gradually, the story came together and a way forward became clearer. It was as if Mel had shone a torch on the problems and helped them work through to an approach that was more likely to work. The team was happy to give Mel the torch and was pleased that he had helped identify next steps. It no longer felt like a dark, dingy cave. The energy of the team went up as they believed there could now be a successful outcome and a way forward.

A torch is a simple device which shines light in a forward direction. Sometimes we can be overwhelmed by the complexity of issues. We see a problem from so many different angles with hundreds of different shadows. A torch shines one beam of light that looks through a problem to the far side.

When the torch is focused on where you want to go, it helps the eyes look forward clearly, uncluttered by the darkness all around. This is not about ignoring the wider context: it is about focusing the torch on what is really important and following that direction and not being distracted by everything else going on around you.

Practical steps

When you are faced with complicated issues, some questions might be:

- If I want to focus on how to find a way through this problem, where would I direct the torch?
- Do I want to hold the torch, or do I want to pass it to someone else who might have greater insight?
- What is the main beam of light I want to show on this problem to help clarify it in my own mind?
- If I wanted a simple, clear solution how might I express that simply?

If you are in a dark place you would shine the torch slowly on one wall or crevice after another. You would not flash it around quickly. Is that an analogy that might help when you are addressing a difficult issue, namely shining the torch slowly and purposefully on each aspect so you can see more clearly how the different elements fit together?

06 RECHARGE YOUR BATTERIES

Don't allow yourself to go flat

Have you ever been caught on a rural road with a flat car battery? You feel isolated and helpless. If a kind motorist stops and uses "jump-start leads" to help start your car, you are relieved that you are now able to reach a place where your battery can be charged. But you are cross with yourself as you had left the lights on, and allowed the battery had run down; you had stalled on a steep hill and been unable to start the engine again.

Recharging our batteries is about taking responsibility for our own energy levels. Our time may be finite, but our energy levels can go up and down. Most of us know what increases our energy and what saps it. But many of us only take partial cognisance of this self-knowledge.

In my book *The Four Vs of Leadership: Vision, Values, Value-added and Vitality*, I suggest that one of the characteristics of successful leaders is that they understand their sources of vitality and unashamedly spend time reinforcing their vitality and energy. If your vitality comes from your family, community, sport, the arts or your faith, how can you spend more time reinvigorating the sources of vitality? This is not about being selfish, it is much more about self-preservation and personal effectiveness.

We ignore at our peril the signals when our batteries are flat. When we feel tired, cross, frustrated, bored or disengaged, it can be time to recharge our batteries. On a busy day, recharging our batteries might be about finding shafts of stillness, walking more slowly between meetings, adopting the smoker's practice of having a five minute break outside, or breathing more slowly.

Finding ways to recharge your batteries is not about escapism. It is cultivating the practice of coming in and out of whatever situation you are in. In order to be fully effective in any situation, it can be a valuable device to sit outside that situation and observe what is going on so that you can re-enter after a few moments' observation of what is going on.

❖ **Rebecca's story:**

Rebecca kept getting home exhausted. The evening consisted of eating, watching television and having a desultory conversation with her partner. Her tiredness did not make her popular at home. Her work was demanding and it was not possible, realistically, to reduce the hours significantly. Her solution was to get into work a bit earlier so she could leave earlier, to do more physical exercise during the day, to drink a lot of water and much less coffee, to deliberately give herself a break of five minutes on a regular basis and to think explicitly, as she walked back to her front door, how she was going to engage the interest of her partner that evening. Changing her routine and building in some more explicit planning had a beneficial effect. She knew that she would need to keep this pattern under review and keep refreshing it, but recharging her batteries was now both a practical as well as a theoretical priority.

Recharging your batteries is about looking after your physical, intellectual, emotional and spiritual well-being. It is seeing your life in many different dimensions and being conscious about the different energy levels and how you can take those levels up or down. It is about stretching your physical activity, keeping up your intellectual interests and stimuli, reinforcing and developing the emotional bonds of friendship, and looking at life from a spiritual as well as utilitarian perspective so that what matters to you most, informs your decisions.

Thriving in your work might also mean stopping certain things which run down your batteries. It might mean spending less time with people who drain your energy and less time on activities which do not give you a sense of making a difference in a sphere that is important to you.

Practical steps

Looking forward over the next few weeks, what practical steps might you take to:

- Recharge your batteries
- Keep them charged
- Stop doing activities which drain your energy

What practical steps might you take to recharge your batteries in terms of your physical well-being, intellectual well-being, emotional well-being and spiritual well-being. Are there two out of these four aspects of well-being which you might take forward with a friend or mentor holding you to account, so that you do make the progress which is important to you?

07 SPOT THE FLICKER

Hope springs eternal

I have worked with leadership teams where there isn't a strong sense of working together as a team. Members say this could never be a successful team. And yet there are sometimes flickers of hope seen in moments of goodwill between different members of the team. My belief is that groups can grow to act as a team and support each other well. It can take a long time for a flicker to turn into a team that glows and performs well together, but sceptics can be converted.

When working as a coach with individuals or groups, I am always looking for the flicker. People will often come with entrenched views and be focused on what they regard as success and failure. They come with a set of competences and ways of doing things that are important to them, but that may or may not coalesce well with the aptitudes and approaches of others.

I sometimes observe a dialogue of the deaf or the grating of wheels where the energy comes from friction rather than from cogs working well together. As a coach you look for the flicker of hope when the eyes begin to look surprised, engaged or hopeful. There is a moment when that sense of "well perhaps" can bring a new sense of possible enlightenment or opportunity.

When you see the flicker, you have to let it grow of its own accord. An initial flicker may be fragile and disappear as quickly as it arrived. The flicker needs to be nurtured and not rushed. It needs to flicker in the breeze and not be blown out by a gust of well-intentioned energy.

A flicker of hope can be about a new idea or approach, or about the possible redemption of a relationship, or a different way of working together, or the potential for a more constructive working relationship. Flickers of hope come out of an awareness that change needs to happen, and the possibility of creating new and renewed alliances and teams that can become more effective if they are willing to work together differently.

❖ Jennifer's story:

Jennifer felt helpless. The team she was working with were at loggerheads with each other. How could she enable them to be more positive and creative together and leave some of their prejudices behind? As a team coach she felt that their expectations were high and their willingness to change their approach was low. She was explicit in playing back to them what she observed which was about distance, edginess, lack of common purpose and individual agendas.

The team's initial reaction was that her comments were high-handed and irrelevant. But they accepted that there was some truth in those comments. What she was looking for was a flicker of acknowledgement that there was an issue to address. As soon as she saw the flicker, she encouraged them gently but firmly to be open about some of their observations and try to build a way forward. Some of the initial steps were small and presentational, but members of the team soon began to change their attitudes which enabled the team to build a stronger foundation for the future.

Spotting the flicker requires patience. It is like waiting for the kingfisher by the riverbank who comes when he is ready and is gone just as quickly. There is a moment when there is a flicker of awareness, that someone is beginning to listen and is open to a new approach. We can be so preoccupied with our own intentions that we fail to see that flicker of interest.

We need to focus on our own intent and be clear about our objectives and our approach, but we need to understand where others are coming from and be open to listening, not just to their words, but also to their physical expressions and body language. When people are ready to open up to a new perspective and move on in their understanding, it will often be clear in their demeanour and their thoughtfulness.

Looking for the flicker is about seeing the glint in someone's eyes when they are ready to move on and are more open to different possibilities.

Practical steps

As you look back, when have you spotted a flicker of interest or understanding in someone who is ready to move on and change their perspective? When has the flicker of interest grown into something much more significant?

Looking forward as you build allies for an approach which you think is important:

- What is the flicker of interest you see in different people?
- What further interest might you kindle in different people?
- How do you maintain that sense of hope which will enable you to ensure steady progress in building a stronger sense of common purpose and shared endeavour?

Spotting the flicker is about combining patience with seizing the opportunity when it arises. But in seizing the opportunity, one needs to be measured and firm, without rushing in and killing the flame.

08 WATCH AGAINST BEING BLINDED

Do not be taken in

The person who talks confidently and smoothly catches our attention. They tell stories which engage our interest. We are attracted by their positive approach and personality. We are excited by their passion for the future.

In the moment we may be engaged, but outside the room we can feel sceptical and question whether we have been "taken in". We can be blinded by enthusiasm or energy. We want to believe that something is possible and sometimes we might even suspend our disbelief in order to enhance the prospect of something we hold dear happening.

An entrepreneur wanted to refurbish some inner city housing and then sell the properties to young professionals. The entrepreneur had a passion for improving the quality of housing stock and for creating a social mix of people in inner city areas. His approach was engaging and persuasive, but he went bankrupt and left a trail of people who felt that the entrepreneur's promise was stronger than his delivery.

Sometimes we want to be blinded! We want to believe something is possible and if someone says it is possible, we will believe in them. But this is a dangerous road to self-delusion. We need to assess continually what we want to believe in and why it stands the test of credibility. We can be blinded by our own desires for success or affirmation.

We can set our aspirations on reaching a particular grade by a particular age and focus all our attention on that goal. In this way, we may become blinded to other opportunities, as well as to the emotional needs of our families and those we love. We may be ambitious for the best of reasons, for example because of our sense of wanting to make a difference, our faith perspective, our belief in the community or a passion to improve the aspirations of adults or children we work with. Ambition based on righteous causes is commendable but can be destructive of an individual's well-being and wider contribution to life.

❖ Avril's story:

Avril wanted to invest her time in the young people she was responsible for as a probation officer. She desired to see hope in their lives. She put huge effort into getting alongside the young people and working with them. But perhaps she was a bit blind to their behaviour. Some of them were on drugs or drinking far too much and did their best to hide this from her. Avril wanted to believe they were reformed characters: she was not wanting to look for signs of drugs and alcohol. They duped her into believing they were fine citizens and she colluded with this without realising her mistake. Her professionalism demanded that she should have looked more critically at the behaviour patterns: in retrospect, she felt cross with herself that she had been taken in.

When we are taken in, we should not beat ourselves up too much. Bringing a positive, encouraging approach in our dealings with people will normally bring out the best in them. Just sometimes, we are taken advantage of and have to accept that we make mistakes. But far better that we believe in people and they let us down, than we give them no chance to demonstrate how they have changed.

Thriving in your work involves being positive about what the people around you can contribute, while at the same time being wary lest you be taken in and duped.

Practical steps

It might be worth reflecting on:

- Who has blinded you in the past with their passion and how did you respond to it?
- How do you best ensure you are not taken in by those who want your support?
- How best do you balance being realistic and at the same time believing that people can change and become reformed characters?

Over the next two or three weeks might you:

- Keep an eye open for when someone looks as if they want to blind you with their latest passion?
- How best do you stay objective when part of you wants to believe that someone has got the ideal solution to a problem you have been wrestling with?

WORK AS A TEAM

We watch a team with admiration when it is working well together. We cheer when a team is playing well, with individuals demonstrating a clear understanding of each other's contributions. A couple playing in a doubles tennis match are a delight to watch when they are responding well to each other and are anticipating each other's moves.

In contrast, a team that is not seeing eye-to-eye and is dysfunctional can rapidly see its performance collapse with recriminations replacing mutual congratulation as the shared language. Effective team work can take a long time to develop, and then be destroyed in a moment of madness.

This section looks at various aspects of working well as a team using military analogies. Successive chapters look at "burying the hatchet", "choosing your weapons", "bringing on the cavalry", "protecting your leader" and "looking after the wounded". Perhaps these analogies will stimulate in you different approaches when reflecting on your contribution to the teams of which you are a part.

09 BURY THE HATCHET

Let bygones be bygones

If you feel that you have been wronged by a colleague in some way, you may want to keep your distance. If you think that trust has been abused, there is a hesitation about working too closely together or letting down your guard.

Trust takes a long time to build up but is easily eroded if a colleague becomes too aggressive, possessive or over critical. If you feel that a colleague is taking advantage of your good will, you may want to respond in a forceful way which puts the individual "back in their place".

An unthinking action or comment from one colleague can so easily lead to an aggressive retort from someone else. What had been a harmonious relationship can quickly become tainted with misunderstanding, with the distancing between the two people meaning that mutual understanding is difficult to re-establish.

Because self-preservation is such a strong instinct, we fight back instinctively if we think someone is taking advantage of us or pushing themselves in front of us in some way.

❖ Delphine's story:

Delphine enjoyed collaboration. She was always on the look out for conversations with colleagues who could see an issue from different perspectives. She was stimulated by dialogue and developed new ways of tackling difficult issues through intense creative conversation. John, a colleague with whom she had shared an idea, began to express this idea as his own proposal, without giving any acknowledgement to Delphine. She felt resentful and stopped talking to John.

But she knew she had to move on. Delphine missed her conversations with John. She wanted to put to one side the wrong she believed had been done to her. She talked openly with John about her reaction to what he had done. As a result, there was a reconciliation. Delphine was able to move on from her resentment and work effectively with John again. She had "buried the hatchet" and was not going to let this incident get in the way of working effectively with her colleague again.

When a colleague causes us grief in one way or another, one reaction may be to hit back; but one strike can lead to another, a ping-pong dialogue on email can make the feeling of hurt or resentment even worse. Instead of retaliating in an aggressive manner, perhaps the first step is to reflect on what is actually going on in our colleague's head and heart. What has caused the action that has created this reaction in us? The more we understand where a colleague is coming from, the better we are able to respond in a way which is appropriate.

When anger, unease or resentment is built up over a period, the ideal solution is a conversation with the individual who has caused that reaction. The most productive context might be an informal setting where you can be open about your feelings and try to build a new, mutual understanding. Initiating such dialogue may make you feel vulnerable as you may be rebuffed. But often the strongest working relationships are those that have gone through a rough patch, with an open dialogue then rebuilding and strengthening the relationship to a point where it is far more effective.

Even when you feel wronged, if you keep the relationship at a positive level, this approach may well in itself change the attitude of your colleague. Behaviours are often mirrored: you can sometimes draw a working relationship to a better place by keeping your attitude positive and ignoring destructive outbursts.

Practical steps

If you currently feel at odds with a colleague, might some of the following steps be relevant?

- Reflect on why their behaviour has been expressed in its current way.
- To what extent have you been part of the problem?
- Would an open discussion be of potential value in clarifying what has happened and finding a constructive way forward?
- How best can you keep positive in your approach, even though you feel undermined by your colleague?
- Does it help to walk out of the situation and then back into it when you are feeling emotionally less rebuffed or drained?

Sometimes "burying the hatchet" requires a symbolic act of moving on. This could be having a beer together, or sharing a joint platform, or celebrating a shared interest or success. A strong sense of moving on is the best way of leaving the hatchet buried deep below.

10 CHOOSE YOUR WEAPONS

And their swords became ploughshares

Armies throughout the centuries have used a multiplicity of weapons. Some are intended to frighten the enemy, others aimed at slowing them down and others at ensuring they do not fight again. Weapons have evolved over time because of stronger metals, the use of gunpowder and the increased sophistication of technology.

Weapons are emotional as well as physical, with warfare being dominated by emotional and political pressure aimed at undermining opponents and destroying their credibility and self-belief. Often the most effective way of winning a battle is to ensure your people are strongly motivated. The power to persuade and influence is the most important weapon in the armoury.

❖ Judy's story:

Judy did not know whether her colleagues in the architectural practice were her friends or her enemies. Sometimes it felt as if she was fighting her colleagues and not the competition in a difficult market. To be successful as an architectural practice they needed to be clear that the weapons they had at their disposal were used to beat the competition and not to destroy each other. The turning point was when Judy and her colleagues acknowledged that the best use of their powers of persuasion was not to beat each other into submission, but to use their skills to persuade potential clients that their architectural approach was by far the best in the market.

Internal dialogue within an organisation that is stimulating and challenging can help you develop and hone your arguments. But like the fighting between two juvenile bears, the intention is to sharpen your own approach and not to destroy your colleague.

When working with an important customer, demonstrating that our approach is more effective than that of our competitors' involves using our weapons in a planned and influential way. If the engagement is hand-to-hand, we need a weapon that is light and flexible. If the engagement is from a distance, we need to make our presence known in a way which is going to hit the target. A dagger is unlikely to be effective if our opponent has a long spear.

When we need to persuade people at a distance, we may have to use megaphone diplomacy. When they are close at hand, we can influence others with a quiet word rather than a loud retort. Choosing your weapons is about finding the best way of engaging both with your colleagues and the apparent enemy. "Who are you fighting?" can be a powerful question in enabling us to be clear about whether too much of our energy is going into destructive conflict with our colleagues rather than into influencing and persuading others effectively.

Practical steps
It might be worth reflecting on:
- Are there weapons you use in a destructive way which can undermine relationships with your colleagues and external contacts?
- Does the language of "choosing your weapons" sound painfully realistic when talking about your colleagues? How might you and your colleagues move on from this destructive situation?
- How might you become increasingly subtle in the way you influence and persuade others?

The most effective weapons are those that are never used. Are there occasions when you might hold yourself back to let others fight it out and exhaust themselves before you suggest a way forward?

What would happen if we used influence and persuasion to build trusting relationships as a means of addressing difficult issues and finding solutions? Sometimes, success comes from leaving the weapons behind and starting a new conversation without a preconceived notion of what success would necessarily look like.

11

BRING ON THE CAVALRY

If you need help, ask for it

We like to win our own battles. We have prepared thoroughly and we believe we are going to succeed. We use all our energy to achieve that objective. If we face opposition and do not make the progress we want, we become even more focused in trying to achieve our objectives.

We can be driven by our own resolution and pride and do not want to be seen to fail. We are determined to keep up our resolve no matter what. We do not want to face the humiliation of failing, and think our reputation and status will be at risk and our long-term future damaged if we do not succeed.

We keep moving faster and faster with the risk of becoming obsessed with achieving a particular goal and failing to see the wider context. Our energy can become sapped through an unremitting focus on a task that is not going well. We need help, but do not want to admit it. Someone else's perspective can be invaluable, but we do not want to show our uncertainty.

The best leaders will always be willing to seek the perspective of other people and think about who else might be able to understand the wider context and bring practical help.

❖ **Rashid's story:**

Rashid was the Operations Director of a small distribution company. He took great pride in the ever-increasing efficiency of the operations. But performance began to slow down and in some areas went backwards. He was determined to solve this problem single-handedly. A couple of other board members offered to help but were rebuffed. Eventually, the Chief Executive insisted that they talked through these issues in some depth as a corporate team and that Rashid brought in external, specialist advice.

Initially reluctant to do this, Rashid accepted that he needed the broader perspective that some of his colleague board members brought and external expertise which drew on the experience of parallel organisations. Rashid was surprised how useful these conversations were. Re-energised and with new ideas, he took steps which led to the efficiency levels going in the right direction again. He was thankful that he had been persuaded to bring in people with different perspectives and skills.

When I was leading the UK Government Department for Education's expansion of nursery education, I was determined to make a success of this expansion and was focused on what we needed to do. The Finance Director persuaded me, against my initial judgement, that I needed a wider base of expertise to draw on. He was right and the policy was developed and implemented successfully. I am forever grateful to my colleague who recognised that I was being obstinate in believing I could do it all by myself with a small team.

Last weekend, my son-in-law and I put up some cupboards in the garage. I knew that doing this on my own would test my skills and would mean that the task would stay on the "to do" list for a long time. My son-in-law has "do-it-yourself" skills that I do not possess. I was delighted to draw on his expertise and enjoy a beer with him while admiring the cupboards now fixed firmly to the wall.

Sometimes we are reluctant to "bring on the cavalry". On other occasions, we are glad to be able to draw on someone else's expertise. A team that is successful is one that draws on the skills and expertise of its members in a dynamic way and brings in external specialist expertise when a wider perspective is needed. But when you "bring on the cavalry", it is important to ensure that they are doing the job you want them to do and not taking over what is yours to decide and deliver.

Practical steps

If you look back over the last few months, how well have you drawn upon the skills and perspectives of your colleagues and external expertise? Looking forward over the next few weeks, when might you:

- Talk to colleagues to understand how they might help you tackle a particular situation?
- Talk to people with similar responsibilities to your own but in a different team or organisation, to get their perspective?
- Bring in external expertise to address particular issues where you could benefit from a perspective or expertise beyond that which you are able to bring?

Knowing when and how to draw on the expertise of others is one of the core strengths of a good leader. Might you redefine what you sometimes see as a weakness in seeking the expertise of others, as a strength?

12 PROTECT YOUR LEADER

Do not dump your woes upwards

It is such a relief to have a leader who will both listen and make decisions. Our ideal may well be to have a leader who both listens and does precisely what we suggest, but we would normally acknowledge that a leader takes into account a wider range of views than just ours alone before making a decision.

It can take a burden off our mind when we judge that we have done our job as well as we can, and it is now up to our boss to make the final decision about the way forward. Such an approach may be ideal for our psychological well-being but it may not be entirely fair on the boss or team leader.

When we have taken on particular responsibilities, they are ours to deliver. It is not fair to the boss to say that we have done our job as well as possible and it is now up to them to decide whether they need to improve it.

Taking responsibility for a piece of work means agreeing with our boss about the outcomes that need to be delivered, and then delivering them. If achieving the outcome becomes a problem, the next steps become a matter for discussion with our boss and not a problem we simply dump on them.

Members of a team have a duty to preserve their leader's energy and time so that the team leader can bring the distinctive value-added contribution that only the boss can bring. It might be that the leader is in the strongest position to negotiate with others both inside and outside the organisation. The boss might have strategic capabilities that the team needs. The last thing that the team needs is for its leader to be weighed down with decisions and issues which can best be taken on by others.

❖ **Vicky's story:**

Vicky had been working in her team within the insurance company for a couple of months. Her boss gave her lots of practical advice which helped Vicky grow in confidence. But Vicky now knew that she had to take responsibility for her own decisions. She was confident in her own judgement and began to seek her boss' advice on far fewer occasions. This helped Vicky's confidence grow, but also meant that more of her boss' time was available to steer the wider direction of the business. Through the mentoring that the boss gave when she first took on this role, she had grown into her job well. At the same time, Vicky also felt a strong sense of responsibility to enable her boss to do his job well by not cluttering his time with small requests which would be more about seeking reassurance than about gathering new insights.

Protecting your leader is also about recognising at an early stage where there might be difficulties across the organisation or with external parties, and trying to handle those issues before they become major problems, before the boss needs to be drawn in.

Protecting your leader might also be about helping your leader guard his time and energy. It could mean not asking for a complicated conversation at 6.45pm or just before the boss has to speak at a demanding, public event. Protecting your boss is about choosing the content, the context and the timing of discussions so they are both productive and enjoyable. You want your boss to be looking forward to discussions with you and not dreading them!

Practical steps

One approach to protecting your leader is to think through the following steps:

- What is the value-add I particularly want from my boss where he can make a distinctive contribution?
- On what issues do I tend to go to my boss where I could and should make the decisions?
- How can I ensure that my boss looks forward to conversations with me rather than dreading them?
- While taking full responsibility for what is in my domain, how do I best keep my boss informed?

Looking ahead to the next week:

- When might I be tempted to dump a problem on my boss?
- How might I get the balance right between personal responsibility and keeping my boss informed?
- What might I do to enable my boss to make their distinctive contribution as effectively as possible?

13

LOOK AFTER THE WOUNDED

You may need help one day

The stark reality from the animal kingdom is that the wounded are often left to die, ostracised and alone. The young are looked after but the injured adult is left to fend for itself. Often, working and living within an organisation can feel like the harsh reality of the animal kingdom.

It is so easy to criticise someone when they make a mistake. Part of our human nature takes pleasure in someone else's misfortune. We say to ourselves that we would never have made that mistake or got ourselves into that difficult situation.

We tend to keep our distance from someone who is beginning to be tainted with failure. We are concerned about the impact on our reputation of being identified with someone who is not doing well.

The risk is, we stand aside at the very moment when a colleague most needs our support and encouragement. What does it take for us to want to be alongside somebody at their time of need? We will readily support and encourage a member of our family or a good friend if things are not going well, but in a work context, our first inclination is often to stand aside. Why? Because we do not want to be tainted with their problem or get sucked into their difficulties or distracted from our priorities.

At present, you may feel fit, able and strong in your work, but as night follows day, you will go through periods of feeling wounded. Your attitude to those who are wounded may not be reciprocated by those same people when you go through a phase of being wounded. Looking after the wounded is not about self-interest. It is based on a duty of care to your colleagues and also about living your life in a manner that is consistent with your values.

It is right to build up a sense of mutual encouragement and support with others so that when you are wounded, there is a willingness to support you. I am hugely indebted to two colleagues who were very important sources of strength for me during a difficult period. Nurturing those people who will support you when you are wounded is an investment that will not be wasted.

❖ Bridget's story:

At the law firm where Bridget worked, the success of the firm was dependent on each partner bringing in a certain amount of business each year. When Bridget saw her figures beginning to slip, her disappointment initially led her to blame other people both outside and inside the organisation. Her mode of fighting back involved alienating others rather than encouraging them to support her. Eventually, when Bridget was willing to admit she needed the support of her colleagues, some of them actually committed time to help her work through next steps in terms of her own business development. Gradually, her confidence came back and stimulating conversations with colleagues took her into new areas of focus. Slowly, her figures began to improve and she was mindful to thank those around her who had helped her get her confidence and creativity back.

Looking after the wounded is sometimes about nurturing them back to full health and strength so that they can play their full part in the organisation. On other occasions, looking after the wounded is about enabling them to come to terms with their injuries or limitations so they can move on to other spheres with honour. Sometimes the wounded do need to be "carried off the pitch" but this must be done in such a way that they are thanked for their contribution and then looked after so that they can move into other spheres successfully.

Practical steps

As you observe those people around you, might it be worth asking:

- Who is wounded and what practical encouragement and support might you give?
- What can you learn from observing the experience of those who have been wounded and are now recovering?
- Who might become wounded in a situation which you could influence so that the wounding is less likely?

In terms of your own experience:

- What are you feeling wounded about and are you allowing that to undermine your confidence?
- With whom do you have a bond of mutual support where a conversation will enable you to move on from feeling wounded?

Perhaps a key for any leader is to be a healer, enabling people to rebuild their strength and learn from their experience. This often hidden role can have a profound effect on the long-term health of an organisation, so that the wounded are not cast adrift but enabled to make a full contribution either in the organisation or in another sphere.

CHOOSE YOUR IMPACT

We often believe our impact is going to be a positive one. We have a preferred style which we use on a regular basis. We think that people will always respond well to our approach and style. We might think it would be disingenuous to vary our style. We want to be true to ourselves and to approaches that have worked well in the past.

But might we become too predictable? If our colleagues always know what we are going to say, our views might be discounted. We might get a reputation for being a "one trick pony" and therefore have a reduced impact on others.

Bringing an approach which is true to your values and preferences on the one hand but also meets the requirements of the situation, is an important balance to reach. We need to be able to choose our impact in a way which is effective but does not look manipulative or inconsistent with our values.

At the heart of choosing your impact is the ability to stand back and see yourself as others see you and to see the wider context in which you are having an influence. This section looks at various aspects of choosing your impact, including: knowing when to put your foot down, watching where you tread, watching out for the kickback and recognising when you have two left feet.

14

KNOW WHEN TO PUT YOUR FOOT DOWN

What matters most to you?

We observe some people being dogmatic. Sometimes we ignore them or we might work round them. Their dogmatism becomes tiresome after a while. It appears they are self-opinionated on everything.

We observe others who express clear views but manage to distinguish between their fixed points and the perspectives which they want to talk through with others. We respect someone who can distinguish between points for debate and fixed points in their thinking or beliefs.

As a project or piece of work develops, you will have clear views about what should happen next. Your previous experience might lead you to think that a particular option is not doable; but do you just assert it is non-viable, or do you set out arguments to support your view that it is unlikely to work? Is your insistence based on reason or emotion?

Sometimes it is right to put your foot down because the expertise you bring determines that a particular approach is not possible for say, legal, auditing or health and safety reasons. But whether your colleagues will agree with you does depend on the respect with which your expertise is held, coupled with a track record of having been proven right before.

Sometimes putting your foot down can be counter-productive. The party you have blocked in can feel poorly treated and that their views were not property considered. Preparing the way is important so that an individual is ready for you to say "no". When you are clear that a particular avenue is not possible, the most effective approach can be to use questions to enable your colleague to reach the same conclusion without your having to insist on your preferred approach.

Often, setting out your preferences, fixed points and the areas on which you do not have a strong view can help create the right dialogue in order to arrive at constructive next steps.

❖ Benjamin's story:

Benjamin was an experienced accountant who had strong views about how best a business plan was created. The team within which he worked was preparing a plan for the coming year. The leader wanted all the participants to own the plan, and therefore its design was not something that he wanted to impose on the team. Benjamin came with very strong views and was in danger of alienating his colleagues.

In a quiet word over coffee, the team leader told Benjamin that he should differentiate much more clearly what were clear requirements and what were his preferences. The team leader asked Benjamin to be clear where he agreed with his colleagues in order to ensure everyone could buy-in to the final design of the business plan. Benjamin thus modified his approach, limiting his strong advocacy to two or three fixed points. The result was that his colleagues were much more amenable to his preferences because he was clearly listening to them. Benjamin got 80 per cent of what he would have liked and all three of the points that were crucial.

The corollary of knowing when to put your foot down is knowing when to lift your foot up. Sometimes it might be more productive to say, "I have changed my mind. I am no longer going to have a particular, fixed perspective. I have listened to the views of others and to the way the market is changing and am willing to change and adjust my position."

It may be important to be alert to where being too insistent can lead to unnecessary argument and the slowing down of progress. There can be a trade-off between reaching the right answer from your perspective, or reaching an answer that is good enough but has the support of others and is arrived at quickly, without wasted energy.

Practical steps

When you look back:

- When have you put your foot down in a way that was counter-productive?
- Who do you observe getting their own way without being overly insistent?
- Do you tend to put your foot down too early or too late?

Looking forward over the next couple of weeks:

- Where do you feel it is right to be insistent?
- Where do you have a clear view about the desired outcome but will use questions to others to try and build a shared view about next steps?
- When might you be inclined to be dogmatic, but find on reflection that it is not necessary to be insistent?

15 WATCH WHERE YOU TREAD

Be mindful when you might 'put your foot in it'

I have thoroughly enjoyed my long-distance walks in the hills of England and Scotland. When the footpath is well-trodden, it is smooth and easy to follow, but on many parts of these walks you have to be careful where you tread.

You have to keep an eye looking to the horizon so you are clear where you are going, and one eye looking at the path to ensure that you keep to the route and do not twist your ankle. Good walkers watch carefully where they tread and adjust their route quickly and effortlessly, while still fully absorbing the landscape and the vistas ahead of them.

If you do not want to risk treading on mud or stepping on a slippery rock then the answer is not to go on hill walks. Part of the adventure of a long-distance walk stems from the unpredictability of the terrain, which means adjusting your route and not being wedded rigidly to a particular length of stride or evenness of surface. Part of the challenge and enjoyment of the hill walk is the variety of terrain and the knowledge that, from time to time, you will 'put your foot in it!' be it a bog, a hidden stream or a deposit from a passing cow.

Working in any organisation, you need to be careful where you tread. There will be sensitivities, and it is good to know where they are. There will be histories and relationships where you can put your foot straight into a problem if unaware of the sensitivities.

Sometimes the importance of a goal is such that you need to keep going and recognise that you need to 'put your foot' into a sensitive area. You will want to be diplomatic and careful about how you approach different situations and what you say to different people, but you will never always get it right. We all make mistakes in our approach and need to adjust as a consequence.

Part of the skill in building long-term relationships is knowing how to respond when you have inadvertently caused an upset or adverse reaction. Acknowledging when your words or approach has caused a problem and working through the reasons for that can build an even stronger working relationship than before.

In the most effective teams there is an acceptance that members will not always put their feet in the right place. Sometimes they will tread on each other's toes. Sometimes their feet will come down very firmly when a softer landing was what was needed.

❖ Marcel's story:

When Marcel joined a new team he knew that the working relationship between some of his colleagues was not straightforward. He needed to build a good relationship with each member of the team but felt that he had to tread warily. Gradually, he began to understand some of the history of some of the working relationships and learned who got on well with whom, and who found some of the working relationships less straightforward. Marcel was careful to build good, practical working relationships which meant he avoided some of the pre-existing difficulties. On one occasion, he did tread on a colleague's sensitive feelings and withdrew rapidly. Within a couple of days he had talked the issue through with the person involved and felt their working relationship was better than ever before.

Watching where you tread is both about choosing the route ahead and about watching where you plant your foot next. Success comes through doing both well, and not being preoccupied with what comes immediately after, at the expense of where you want to be in an hour's time.

Practical steps

As you look forward over the next couple of weeks, how best do you:

- Keep a long-term perspective and get the next steps right?
- Accept that the path ahead might not always be smooth going, with potholes and crevices to be overcome?
- Get the balance right between being adventurous in trying out new approaches, and being cautious about where you might make a mistake and not get it "right first time"?
- Recover when you have "put your foot in" a problem without realising you were entering a complicated situation?

16 WATCH OUT FOR THE KICKBACK

Know how you protect yourself

When you have done something well, some of your colleagues will want to congratulate you and express support for what you have been doing. But sometimes, your success is not met with delight by your colleagues.

Every organisation contains an element of competitiveness. Sometimes it is overt and sometimes it is well hidden. How do you best minimise the risk of kickback and handle it when it happens? Kickback or resentment is most likely to occur when trust between people is fragile. Time invested in building good quality working relationships is rarely wasted. Where a relationship is established which includes both positive feedback and encouragement to adapt and grow, it is far less likely that there will be competitiveness of a damaging nature.

Part of coping with the kickback from a colleague is being prepared and knowing when that is likely to happen. Having eyes in the back of your head can be useful. For instance, if you are taking forward a new initiative, being aware of who is likely to support it and who might oppose it can be helpful in knowing where critical comments are going to come from.

❖ **Julian's story:**

Julian enjoyed being part of a group of engineers. He thought there was a strong sense of mutual support within the group. After a busy year he received a bonus which was larger than that of his colleagues. Somehow, they found out how much his bonus was. They congratulated to him to his face but were less fulsome behind his back. They felt their efforts had not been fully rewarded. His colleagues went through a period of not being as supportive and they left him out of some important conversations. Julian felt that he was experiencing a kickback from his colleagues because of his bonus. He decided not to protest. He continued to be very open and friendly to his colleagues and work jointly with them. It did not take long for his colleagues' apparent resentment to wither away. They were soon the best of colleagues again. Julian was glad that he had not made a fuss over their reaction to his bonus and had been patient.

How best do you respond if someone kicks back at you? It may be that the individual is unaware of his behaviour. Often, frustration can affect someone's demeanour without their deliberately wanting to kick back at an individual. Also, if something happens to distance a relationship with a colleague, it might appear that there is a kickback when it is just that colleague feeling a bit more distanced from you.

At the other extreme, someone might backstab you by criticising you and undermining what you have done. At one stage in my career I felt undermined by a colleague. My mistake was to ignore what the colleague did rather than have a conversation with him. My only comfort was that this person was undermining others too, and got a reputation for underhanded behaviour which, in the long run, did him no good at all.

When people are driven by ambition they can be blatantly two-faced. They can be expressing words of praise to you one day and damming criticisms to a third party the next day. Always keep an eye on those who are ambitious, and watch your own ambition so it does not distort the way you behave in relation to other people. Maintaining consistency in working relationships is a bedrock for a team working well together. Energy levels will go up and down but a consistent level of trust will reduce the likelihood of destructive behaviour between individuals.

Practical steps

It might be worth reflecting on:

- Who might want to kick back at you and why?
- What is your reaction if someone is critical about you behind your back?
- How best do you build the type of working relationships that will minimise the likelihood of insidious personal criticism?

Looking forward over the next couple of weeks:

- When might you be inclined to kick back and how will you handle it?
- Who might be critical of you and how might you forestall that criticism?
- Who might knife you in the back and how would you handle that?

17
RECOGNISE WHEN YOU HAVE TWO LEFT FEET

Watch over-reliance on one skill

We try to build a reputation by being good at a variety of activities. We want to excel in a range of ways. Sometimes we do not want to admit we are good at certain aspects of the job and less so at other aspects. We may be good at oral communication but find certain forms of written communication draining and time consuming.

A starting point is being honest about what we do well, what we do less well and agreeing with our boss and colleagues about how our aptitudes can be used to optimal effect while our less-strong areas are either developed or complemented by the skills of others. If we can kick well with our left foot but not with our right, how best can we serve the team by using our left foot? The key to success is honesty and transparency about skills, coupled with teams working well together to use each person's skills to best effect.

The phrase "having two left feet" implies clumsiness and an uncertainty of touch that is amusing to others. Avoiding clumsiness is about effective preparation and training and being aware of your impact on others.

The person who jokes about having "two left feet" is acknowledging to themself and others what they are good at and what they are less good at. Being honest with ourselves about our limitations is an important first step to using our skills well and understanding our limitations.

Sharing this truth with others in an open way allows a team to gel well together, without them having to pretend that someone is good at something when that it is one of their less strong areas.

❖ Henry's story:

Henry had a tendency to say whatever came to his mind. In the midst of an important and difficult meeting he would often make comments that were tangential. Sometimes he could be rude without realising he was being offensive. His defence was that he was being honest, but his frankness often created a discordance that was at odds with reaching a positive outcome which everyone would accept.

Henry knew that he could destroy a productive meeting with careless talk. He was aware that he needed to modify his approach and became better at recognising when he could disrupt a conversation. His points may be technically valid but if they destroyed the flow and undermined an emerging conclusion, then he was being entirely unhelpful!

One of the organisations I worked for had a sports day once a year. One year I entered the three-legged race where my left foot was strapped to my colleague's right foot. We knew that to succeed in the race my left leg and my colleague's right leg had to act as one. After a few minutes' practice, we were ready for the race. When we disciplined our feet to run in harmony with each other, we did well. If we were slightly out of sync with each other, we fell over.

When we run, the right and left legs have to act in time with each other. If they are not in a rhythm we cannot run successfully. If one foot has been slightly injured, it affects both feet until they find a new rhythm to operate well together. If it feels as if we have two left feet, you may have to strengthen your right foot so that we can participate in a coherent way rather than just hobbling on the left foot. Alternatively, you may decide on the three-legged race, where your right leg is strapped together with the strong left leg of a colleague, so that together, you can achieve more than you would have done on your own.

Practical steps

It might be helpful to reflect on:

- Who do you observe to have two left feet? What do you learn from the best and worst parts of their impact?
- In what situations do you tend to get your balance wrong and end up lop-sided in your contribution?
- Who best can you team up with so that you can go forward effectively together?
- How can effective preparation and training enable you to be less reliant on one set of skills?

Your impact may be very good when you use your left foot. A key question is how do you keep balance while moving forward when you are relying on one particular attribute or skill for your success.

DEVELOP NEW SKILLS

We admire the skill of an athlete, author or speaker as we observe the smooth way in which they express their skills. It looks so easy, and yet it always results from much hard work and preparation. We take pride in the skills we possess, be they about technical competence or emotional sensitivity or physical prowess.

Sometimes thriving in our work is about developing skills that might not seem so essential. We can berate ourselves if we forget key information, such as someone's name. Yet learning how to forget is a crucial skill. We like to build predictability and certainty, yet the ability to see round corners and spot the invisible is so precious.

Life is full of activity and we can so easily ignore the skill of being able to lay still and be silent. So much emphasis is placed on getting it right the first time, we forget that acknowledging when you are wrong is a sign of strength and not weakness.

18

LEARN HOW TO FORGET

The more I forget, the more I remember

We admire people who have an excellent memory and we pass knowing glances if someone is being forgetful. We may refer to "senior moments" when we cannot remember an individual's name.

But the ability to forget is a precious skill that needs to be cherished and not dismissed. How good are we at forgetting? Forgetfulness can be dangerous when we have made commitments to others and have obligations to meet, but the skill of forgetting can be a strength when it allows new information, thoughts and ideas to enter your mind, unimpeded by material that is best forgotten. The more we forget, the more we can remember!

❖ Jane's Story

Jane kept chastising herself for forgetting what she regarded as key information. Gradually, she came to accept that as long as she knew how to access the information, that was fine. Jane allowed herself the licence to forget which gave her a new sense of liberation and the mental space to absorb new issues and not be burdened by little used facts.

We can be caught in a time warp when we believe there is only one way of doing things. Sometimes for our own preservation we have to "wipe the slate clean" so that we can start again and think in new and different ways. The ability to forget is central to moving on and thriving. If we remembered every car number plate we had ever read, our mind would be completely cluttered. We need to forget facts to allow room for new facts to be remembered.

The skill of forgetting is also about our emotional reactions. Sometimes our minds can be cluttered with emotion, anger or frustration about past events. We can feel we have been unfairly treated by our organisation (resentment), we have not been able to achieve what we hoped (frustration) or that we have been treated badly by a particular leader (anger).

We can be haunted by past failures which limit our confidence to succeed in future projects. The baggage we carry can slow us down and diminish our aspirations.

Emotional clutter in our minds can be a damaging inhibitor. We get stuck and are unable to move on. Our emotions can become so fixed or frazzled that our scope for freshness has gone.

Liberation can come through recognising our emotional reactions and reflecting on how best we can leave them behind. When we are honest about the anger, resentment or frustration that is gnawing away at us, we can begin to make progress. Sometimes we need to box a negative emotion, talk it through with a good friend or decide on the best way to try and leave it behind and move on.

The skill of forgetting is about recognising that the past is in the past. It is de-cluttering our mind of irrelevant facts and destructive emotions and then giving ourselves the space to be open to new experiences. Forgetting well is linked to developing a selective memory that deletes the irrelevant and dated, while retaining both eternal truths and new wisdom.

Practical steps

Some practical ways of increasing your skill of forgetting might include the following. In terms of forgetting facts:

- Be willing to blank out blocks of information
- Know when you can rely on others for factual information
- Take pleasure in what you cannot now remember rather than feeling it is a failure!

In terms of forgetting unhelpful emotional reactions, practical steps might include:

- Write down a difficult or painful memory and then put the piece of paper through a shredder or rip it into small pieces
- Box a particular memory in your mind and then metaphorically throw the box over a cliff
- View a particular experience as a dark cloud and then watch the dark cloud gradually float away and diminish in size
- Try to see the potential benefit that has come from an experience which you regard as negative
- Encourage friends to give you positive feedback when they see you move on from resentment, anger or frustration

Celebrate when you forget! Remembering is important when someone needs to be thanked and encouraged, but forgetting can be even more important when it is time to move on in your thinking and leave behind facts and clutter that are proving to be unhelpful, dangerous or destructive. What might you now resolve to forget?

19

SEE ROUND CORNERS

The more I look round the bends, the further I see ahead

We admire those who are confident about the future. We can be in awe of their single-mindedness and determination. We can feel that life would become so much simpler if we could adopt some aspects of their clarity and vision.

But perhaps uncertainty needs to be cherished and not feared? If there is lack of clarity perhaps this will help us to think more clearly and work through issues in a step-by-step way. If the future was clear with no uncertainties, we would happily move forward and potentially become blinkered to the world around us. It is only when the way ahead looks less than clear that we may be ready to see round corners and look out for other possibilities.

❖ Harry's story

Harry's boss was clear that the business was going to keep expanding. Harry wanted to believe his boss' optimism but brought a cautiousness that he wanted to test. He looked at what the competition was doing and the way the market was likely to go. He talked to different customers to see what their expectations were of the future. Harry could see opportunities for the business, if it changed direction. Gradually, he fed in different ideas to his boss and after steady persistence, persuaded his boss that a change of direction was needed. It was Harry's willingness to look round corners, and then his persistence in putting forward his perspective, that enabled the business to grow. It grew because he changed direction, rather than kept on its original course.

We can become so wedded to a particular approach or point of view. What has worked so well for us in the past, we assume that the same will always be successful in the future. But life is never that predictable. Expectations change: what has wowed people in the past may bore them in the future.

Being utterly single-minded is a great strength in many situations. When preparing for a major race, or leading a specific project, or taking a specific percentage out of the budget, single-mindedness is a huge strength. Using clarity of direction to block out the irrelevant and the trivial can be a key skill. But when it becomes a blinkering that causes new information and new perspectives to be ignored, then single-mindedness can be an individual's undoing rather than their triumph.

What might seeing round corners mean? It can be about understanding the perspective of those who have trod the path before, being aware of what might be the blind alleys, sensing what might be roadblocks along the way, and recognising when shortcuts might be helpful and which of them might be dangerous.

Seeing round corners can involve observing the wider landscape, being conscious of what is visible and what is hidden, reflecting on others' experiences so that you can anticipate the likely consequences of taking different routes, or being willing to climb up to a different viewpoint to survey the landscape ahead.

At the core of being willing to look round corners, is a belief that uncertainty is helpful rather than unhelpful. It is accepting that the unpredictable is always with us and that living with uncertainty is part of the stimulus and excitement of life and work. If every school class lesson was predictable then life as a teacher would become dull.

Uncertainty gives us the stimulus to want to look round corners, to adapt our approach and to make our own decisions about our priorities and attitudes.

Practical steps

Some practical ways of developing the skill of looking round corners might include:

- See an unexpected bend in the way ahead as an opportunity and not a threat
- Don't expect the way ahead to be clear and direct; anticipate rather than fear bends in the road
- Be willing to look ahead and deliberately anticipate what might be the corners you will need to turn

When it comes to a particular blockage in the course you have set yourself, practical steps might include:

- Be clear why you set out on a particular direction, be realistic why the blockage has appeared
- Be willing to think through changes of direction you had not previously anticipated
- Be willing to recalibrate what outcomes you would be content to live with
- See the ability to explore different routes forward as a strength and a weakness
- Enjoy taking the blinkers off and living with uncertainty

Allow yourself to take delight in seeing round different corners; and then in the light of new information and new perspectives, be ready to move forward with a new clarity, at least until the next bend in the road.

20 LAY STILL

Do nothing to change the world

We admire people who are always taking action. We are impressed by their decisiveness, energy, determination and resolve. They always seem to know the right answers or at least they are always willing to debate what the right answer is.

The activity we admire in others can be about action or words or even confident body movements. The assertive movement of the arm or the focused look can give a powerful impression of being in control.

Perhaps a crucial skill is to lay still and be silent. The ability to be quiet in mind, body and spirit is a skill to be treasured and not dismissed. Having an internal stillness and being able to convey a sense of calm to others is a skill that can be underrated in the heat of a busy moment.

❖ Sunil's story:

Sunil was leading a major project where the client was being demanding about what had to be achieved on a particular time scale, and holding rigidly to specific milestones.

Sunil was clear that the final delivery date would be met, but there was a relentlessness about the client's approach that afforded few opportunities to reflect on how the project was going and what adjustments were needed. Sunil was clear that he needed to create space for himself and his team to think carefully about how to progress in the project. They needed space to be still, to consider quietly and thoughtfully what was now needed. They took half a day away from the project and ended up with clarity about key priorities, with other issues relegated to second order. They returned from the time away much more confident about their own future progress, with Sunil now more able to deal with the demanding client.

======

Being still has both internal and external expressions. Being still internally is about being comfortable in yourself, understanding the pace at which you work best and being quietly confident in the approach you are bringing. Internal stillness is about a calmness that comes partially through your emotional make-up and partly through learnt behaviour. Knowing how to step inside and outside situations emotionally can give a perspective which is so precious in keeping cool and objective whatever the situation.

External calmness can be transmitted to others. Panic spreads like an infection. The demeanour that you bring will be mirrored by others. Where our tone is one of agitation, those around us will also become agitated. When we look frustrated, they will become frustrated too. When we come to a situation with a sense of calm purposefulness, that is likely to be a strong signal about the appropriate sort of behaviour.

Sometimes we can be at our most influential when following the thrust of a conversation and then adding to the ideas suggesting ways forward. Being silent can allow us to observe a conversation and then intervene at a key moment. The participant who has been still can often contribute a summary or a reflection that crystallises what has happened and help a conversation change direction. When someone has been still for a while, the other participants may want to know their views which will help create an opportunity to influence.

There are times when some people need to keep talking through their ideas before they will be open to listen to others. Timing is everything in choosing the moment to intervene. Rushing in may well be counter-productive. Waiting for a gap, and then entering a conversation and slowing the conversation down can create a defining moment in the way a meeting is going.

Doing nothing can be absolutely the right thing to do. Intense activity may be irrelevant or wasted effort. Biding your time could be the right answer.

Practical steps

Some practical ways of increasing your skill of laying still might include:

- Practise being quiet and allowing your inner thoughts to dominate your thinking rather than external noises
- Give yourself gaps between meetings, even for a few seconds by walking more slowly
- Be conscious about what helps you be calm and allow that calmness to show

Can you think of current or forthcoming situations where a key skill will be to lay still? In that situation:

- What will help you keep calm and demonstrate calmness?
- What will help restrain you from rushing in too quickly?
- How best will you pace yourself when you are under pressure from other people?

Do enjoy those moments when you decide to lay still. Smile to yourself that doing nothing is sometimes the best way to change the world. Practise the art of timing so you become attuned to intervene at moments when you can have the greatest impact. Do not let yourself be intimidated by those for whom silence or stillness seems to be an alien state of mind.

21

ACKNOWLEDGE WHEN YOU ARE WRONG

*When you show your vulnerability,
you build your inner strength*

We admire those who do not make mistakes. They have an aura of success which makes us believe that everything they do works well. We respect them, but may not be motivated by them.

Admitting that you were wrong may seem a sign of weakness. But showing vulnerability often leads to a growing level of respect and admiration. It is as we show our vulnerability that we build inner strength for the future.

❖ **Hazel's story:**

Hazel believed that her team could complete an important assignment within two weeks. She made a firm commitment and believed her reputation depended on delivering that commitment. With a few days to go to the deadline she realised that this time scale was now not attainable. Her first reaction was to want to hide! Her second reaction was to reach an agreement with her team about what timetable could be attained. Then she explained carefully to her client what the problems had been and when the project could now be delivered with a much greater level of certainty. Her measured approach worked well with the client who accepted the reasons for the change in time scale. By acknowledging the reasons for the change to the client, and being open about the problem, Hazel felt much better able to deal with similar issues in the future.

We plan the steps in a timetable carefully. We do not mean to be foolhardy in saying what can be achieved. But the timetable gets disrupted for unexpected reasons. However hard we try to get back on time, the original time scale is not going to be met. Our first reaction is one of horror or disbelief. We do not like to fail to deliver on our commitments. We do not like to be wrong in our judgements, but sometimes that is life and we have to live with it.

We all make mistakes. If we did not make mistakes, we would not learn. Mistakes are an essential part of refining our approach so we minimise the times when we are unsuccessful in the future.

When inventors create a new product, they can either be described as having failed 1,000 times before they make a successful invention, or their experience can be described as 1,000 successful experiments demonstrating how not to create a particular product. Every failed experiment gives us valuable new data about ourselves and our situation.

When people acknowledge that they were wrong, they are exposing themselves to criticism. If they are public figures the media may latch onto their admission of guilt and castigate them as a result. It is not surprising that many leaders are reluctant to admit that they were wrong because of the media criticism that they are likely to receive.

But when leaders admit their mistakes and come clean on why they were subsequently persuaded to take a different view, their level of influence can go up sharply. Admitting that they have changed their mind is a demonstration that they have been willing to listen. The consequence is that the level of trust they engender with other people is likely to go up rather than down.

However, someone who changes their mind on a regular basis is likely to see their credibility sink without trace. Being willing to acknowledge you are wrong and change your mind is not about flitting from one view to another. It is about considered reflection and changing your view in the light of new information and perspective.

Successful leaders are able to balance effectively being resolute and adaptable. Being resolute is being clear about your course of action, but being adaptable means that you can change your course. Sometimes being adaptable involves just an adjustment; on other occasions it is about a frank admission that you were wrong.

Practical steps

Some practical ways of developing the capacity to acknowledge you were wrong might include:

- Observing when other people admit they are wrong and increase rather than reduce their credibility
- Being more willing to admit your own mistakes and show vulnerability and see what the consequences are
- Observing how you respond when colleagues admit they are wrong

In a particular situation where you think you are in the wrong, what might your next steps be in terms of:

- Being honest about your sense of vulnerability
- Describing your change of view
- The reaction you want other people to have in response to that admission
- How you will build new bridges with those who might be uneasy about or critical of your change of perspective

It is a fascinating paradox that building your inner strength can flow from admitting you were wrong. If we show our vulnerability and our willingness to learn, people may be more willing to follow us. If we treat people with kindness and respect when they show vulnerability we are more likely to elicit that same response when we show vulnerability.

RECOGNISE YOUR EMOTIONS

Our emotions provide us with valuable data and forewarn us of problems. They stimulate us to develop the energy we need to get through difficult situations. Our emotions provide us with life, colour, energy and hope.

Our emotions can be a catalyst for action, or a stimulus for new thinking, or the cause of new alliances. But our emotions can also be our downfall if we are captured by them and become preoccupied with ourselves and our individual needs. Following our emotions can take us into a spiral of depression, or into a new sense of engagement. The choice is ours.

This chapter looks at recognising and handling our emotions in specific areas. It covers becoming a victim, emptying your mind, boxing the gremlins, recognising when you are about to snap and watching when friendships can either enhance or diminish your ability to thrive in your work.

22

DO NOT BECOME A VICTIM

Watch when you feel hard done by

You feel let down, ignored or abused. You have not been treated properly. Somehow you are being made to suffer because of the actions or attitudes of other people. It does not seem fair. Nothing is "going my way", and whatever you do goes wrong. They are not giving you any opportunity to show what you can do.

Have you ever felt any of these emotions? You begin to feel frustrated and cross. You start to feel a victim, persecuted by others with no opportunity to get redress. You interpret every little criticism as further persecution. Even when no criticism is intended you hear words as if they were critical. There is resentment building up inside you which can boil over when someone presses the wrong button.

When a friend says to you, why do you feel frustrated, you pour out your tale of woe. If they dare ask if you are feeling like a victim you protest and say they have joined your critics!

❖ George's story:

George felt that he had been badly treated at work. He had narrowly missed out on a promotion and then only received a modest bonus. He felt that he was being taken advantage of. He always worked hard but began to feel that he was not fully appreciated. Whenever his boss did not say thank you, he felt that he was being criticised.

George felt increasingly frustrated. When a good friend asked whether he was feeling a victim, George's first reaction was to protest while beginning to recognise that there was some truth in the comment. Gradually, he accepted that no one was maligning him or targeting him unfairly. His time for promotion would come, just not yet.

Lots of different stimuli can lead us to feel hard done by. We work actively on a project and do not get the acknowledgement we feel we deserve. We put a lot of focus on encouraging someone to change their mind, and they never admit that we have been influential upon them. We do the groundwork for an important event, and our boss takes all the credit. We work conscientiously to complete a paper for an important meeting, which then falls off the bottom of the agenda.

Life is full of one frustration after another. Shrugging our shoulders and moving on may not be easy. The danger is that one frustration is piled upon another, our energy is sapped, we feel exhausted, got at, undermined, down-trodden and perhaps even worthless.

Frustration can lead to creativity as we find ways around a problem. Even resentment can be constructive if it leads us to correct an unfairness. But when we begin to feel like a victim, the consequences are only destructive.

When we feel a victim we can feel locked in a cage. We can end up expressing negative emotions to those committed to our well-being and stretching their goodwill to the limit. Our objectivity can become completely blurred when we interpret the actions of others in a consistently negative way, even when that is not their intention.

We can get to the point of enjoying being a victim and indulging in the sense that life has treated us unfairly. Perversely, satisfaction can come from enjoying the sense of being persecuted. How many careers and marriages have been destroyed because of indulging in being a victim?

Practical steps

When you begin to feel a victim, practical steps can include:

- Recognise the patterns you have experienced before
- Acknowledge to yourself that you are beginning to feel a victim
- Talk through your reactions with trusted friends asking them to help lift you out of this sensation

If you are currently facing a situation where you may be at risk of feeling a victim, can you:

- Define the risk and identify the causes
- Be clear about what practical steps you might take so you do not slip into becoming a victim
- Engage constructively with those who you feel might be the cause of your feeling a victim

Being alert to our emotions is very important. Recognising when a particular emotion is beginning to grab hold of you means now is the moment to stand back. It can sometimes be helpful to ask yourself what your reaction will be if you are unsuccessful in getting a job or winning a project. Preparing for an adverse reaction can be very helpful in reducing the risk of becoming a victim.

23

EMPTY YOUR MIND

Create space to be open to new insights

Your mind is buzzing. New data is available all the time. You are constantly getting new information off the internet. You want to hear views of different people. Your mind feels flooded with information, views and emotions.

You begin to feel weighed down by this weight of information. It feels like there are lead weights attached to your brain. You want to break free and think new thoughts, but with every turn you take, there are new facts and new opinions. You want to cast yourself adrift from this mountain of information, but at the same time you are attracted to it and want to pick out information you like to use to validate your preferred ways forward.

How do you empty your mind so that you can think your own thoughts and not feel dumped on by the views of others? How do you enable your creativity to blossom, while being informed and enabled by the information available to you and not swamped by it?

❖ Janette's story:

Janette was addicted to the internet. She accumulated information on any subject under the sun. She could give you a sequence of facts on any current topic, and felt that her credibility was based on the knowledge she held. But her friends began to ignore her as they were intimidated by her knowledge and a touch frustrated by her inability to see beyond the factual and into some of the trends or emotions. Gradually, Janette accepted that she needed to leave a bit more space in her own mind and in her conversation. It was only as she de-cluttered her thinking that she was open to hear the views of others and re-enter constructive conversation.

Many of us have memories of preparing for exams. We wanted to fill our minds with information which we can spill out onto the examination paper. Preparing for exams often seemed like garnering more and more information, and yet the best preparation may be to empty your mind prior to an exam so you can think clearly and respond to the questions asked.

When going for an interview information is important, but not too much information. I remember going for various, unsuccessful interviews when I deluged the panel with information. When I help people to prepare for interviews I encourage them to stand back, to sift their knowledge and understanding and be clear about what the key points are that need to be addressed.

If a room is full of furniture there is no space to move the furniture around and create different combinations and different atmospheres. When our minds are full it can be difficult to link insights and trends together. It is only as we empty our minds that we become fully equipped to be creative and have new energy to solve problems in different ways.

Emptying our minds can feel risky as we feel vulnerable to being caught out by not having the latest views on subjects on which we pride ourselves of being well informed. Empty mindedness is not something we do.

When we empty our mind we can be surprised by the thoughts that enter our heads. Initially, the void is filled by the irrelevant, tasks that we failed to do, or emotions that can captivate us. Sometimes emptying our mind is something we avoid doing because the emotions that flood in can feel selfish or destructive.

Perhaps there is a second phase after we have emptied our mind when we become bored with our initial emotions and begin to relax into a space of calmness. When our mind is empty it can be easier to link together different aspirations, expectations and emotions. We can understand more readily why we feel strongly about some of our hopes and fears.

If the perspective we want to bring in our reflection is one of hopefulness and a desire to build a sense of shared endeavour, then we are more likely to make progress than if we allow ourselves to be consumed by gloom and despondency. If we can allow ourselves to be hopeful, then the creativity in that empty space is more likely to be productive. This is not about self-delusion, it is about creating the right context to be constructive.

Practical steps

When our thinking is distorted by buzzing in our mind, practical steps can include:

- Switching into a different type of activity or moving to a different, physical space
- Believing that our insights are more important than information

When you are able to empty your mind what might you want to encourage your thinking to embrace? What might you want to stimulate in terms of:

- Signs of hope
- The linking together of different insights
- Space for creativity and new approaches

24 BOX THE GREMLIN

Can we tame the gremlin most of the time?

Sometimes we are confident, bright and assertive. On other occasions we can be racked with self-doubt and fears. Our emotions can sway surprisingly quickly from elation to exasperation. On other occasions we cannot escape doubts and fears that take hold upon us and will not let us go.

Doubts keep bubbling up and appear randomly, rather like bubbles at a hot pool. Doubts or fears can feel like a gremlin jumping from one shoulder to another, whispering discouragement into our ears. How best do we recognise our doubts and fears and contain them up to a point and live with their effect on us?

❖ Gloria's story:

Gloria always felt inadequate when working with particular colleagues. They seemed much more confident and assertive than her. In their presence Gloria seemed to become nervous, uncertain and hesitant in her contributions. Even the sound of the voices of some of her colleagues brought to the surface feelings of inadequacy. She was afraid of making a fool of herself and receiving their disapproval. She imagined putting this fear of disapproval in a cardboard box and fixing the lid firmly on the box. She could hear the fear trying to get out, but the image of the fear in the box helped her limit its negative effect on her. She taught herself to make useful contributions with this group of colleagues, while recognising that she would never feel entirely at home in their presence.

Fears come in all shapes and sizes. Some are rational and others, illusory. Some fears are helpful. If we are concerned that a meeting may not go well, a touch of fear can help us prepare effectively, but too much fear and the preparation becomes obsessive and its impact forced and laboured. We may doubt our own competence or confidence. The spectre of previous occasions when all has not gone as we would have wanted may become a limiting factor in how we position our own contribution.

The strategy we use to box our doubts or fears will vary among individuals, depending on our personality, our history and our preferences. For some, the best antidote is to remember when we have overcome doubts or fears on previous occasions. Memories of successful pieces of work or interventions in our mind can be a valuable reinforcement that "we can do it". For others it is holding in our mind different pictures of success or calmness which stabilises us and enables us to address our doubts and fears. What can help in coping with doubts or fears is to be mentally in two parallel existences, whereby the pressures of the work day are set alongside our delight in friendships or experiences outside the work environment.

A technique that some find helpful is to imagine the doubt or fear as a gremlin sitting on your shoulder with whom you can have a conversation. The gremlin might be trying to drip poison in your ear about your competence or confidence. You might smile back at the gremlin, thank it for its thoughts and then put it firmly in a box where he can chunter away to limited effect. For some the mental picture of throwing the box over the edge of a cliff can be helpful. For others the picture of the gremlin chuntering away in a cardboard box is more helpful as doubts and fears may be containable but are unlikely to be eradicated.

Living with our doubts and fears is part of life. It is often a consequence of the way we are made, and to pretend that we can radically change ourselves can only lead to disappointment. But with experience of different situations and the support of trusted others we can devise methods that allow us to live with ourselves and contain the doubts and fears, without pretending that they will ever be completely removed.

Practical steps

Some practical ways of containing doubts and fears might include:

- Be honest with yourself about those doubts and fears
- Remember how you have overcome them in the past
- Develop a strategy for diminishing their impact, one step at a time

If you are currently dealing with a particular doubt or fear:

- What are the practical next steps you might take?
- Who are the trusted others with whom you can work through this doubt or fear?
- Might it be helpful to box that fear or doubt to contain its impact?
- How best might you continue to live with that doubt or fear?

When we feel a doubt or fear there can be a temptation to "beat ourselves up". But doubts and fears are a natural part of life. They come and go. The challenge is how we contain them and tame them, recognising that removing them entirely is likely to be unrealistic.

25

RECOGNISE WHEN YOU ARE ABOUT TO SNAP

Be alert to when you are close to the edge

We pride ourselves on our calmness and our rational approach. We are conscious when we become annoyed and are able to work with that emotion. But sometimes we recognise that we can come close to the edge and might show annoyance or anger in a way that is counter-productive.

What do we do when we sense a strong, emotional reaction rising up in us? When do we let it out or contain it? When do we go into avoidance mode and move into another space? Or when do we acknowledge to those around us how we are feeling about a particular situation?

❖ **Len's story:**

Len had prepared a careful project plan. He had talked to all the interested parties and felt he understood their perspective. He knew the direction in which he wanted to proceed and was determined not to be derailed. Then he met with a group of colleagues, some of whom had not read his paper and were asking irrelevant questions, others seemed to be being gratuitously critical, and there were also those who did not seem to care. Len felt himself getting rattled. He was close to expressing indignantly that his project paper was not being taken seriously. He decided to refrain from that initial reaction and suggested that he had a conversation individually with each of his colleagues to brief them on his approach and so that he could understand their perspectives better. By the time of the next meeting, they were all in full agreement about next steps. His cautious approach had been right:

if he had snapped at his colleagues the risk would have been that the project could go backwards.

We each have a threshold beyond which we can become agitated and potentially angry or aggressive. Most of us we know when this about to happen.

What causes us to snap might be the behaviour of others, the pacing of a particular discussion or project, our own well-being, the quality of the relationship with our colleagues, or the expectations from others.

It can be useful to assess ourselves before a particular day or meeting on the risk of slipping into agitation or anger. Perhaps when the risk is higher, our own observation of ourselves becomes the more important in terms of being conscious of when we could flip over into dangerous territory.

When we reach a point where we might express agitation or anger, practical techniques that can be useful include physically moving in our seat, getting a cup of coffee or going to the washroom. The smoker's technique of a five-minute break in the fresh air can be a valuable antidote.

With people we know well, explaining why you feel agitated or angry in a dispassionate way will normally be more helpful than expressing the agitation or anger. Those who know you well will want to understand the causes of the emotion. For those who know you less well, it can be a good starting point for a discussion about how you can work together effectively.

If they boil up too much inside us, agitation and anger will be corrosive to ourselves and our relationships with others. At the same time these emotions are giving us valuable information about ourselves and the situation we are in. When we feel agitated it may be because we have good reasons why a particular course of action is misconceived. The skill is in turning that agitation into an approach and dialogue which is going to have a constructive effect.

When you want to "throw something" or "kick the door" perhaps the right thing to do is to go outside and throw something. On other occasions it might be a step you imagine taking without actually doing so. Throwing a colleague out the window is likely to be a career limiting act. Mentally visualising the act of throwing someone out the window is certainly the lesser of two evils!

When visiting a coastline it is a delight to walk along the cliffs, enjoying the views and the sight of the sea breaking on the rocks. But we know that going too close to the edge of a cliff is dangerous and is something we avoid doing. As we push the boundaries in developing new ideas or building dialogue with different groups of people, we may sense when we get close to the edge and our patience is being tested. That is likely to be the right moment to withdraw from the edge so we are not blown over by a gust of unexpected wind.

Practical steps

Some practical ways of enhancing your ability to know when you are about to snap:

- Be conscious of what situations or people most agitate you
- Understand what are the emotions within you that are likely to lead to agitation or anger
- Understand the patterns in your own well-being about when you are most at risk of agitation or anger

Can you think of a forthcoming situation where you may be at risk of being near the edge or snapping? How best might you handle that situation in terms of:

- Preparing yourself with the right information and expectations
- Recognising where other people are coming from
- Being clear what your boundaries are and how far you are willing to be pushed

• Knowing your escape mechanisms if you feel you might snap

There are moments when each of us feel agitation or anger as these are basic emotions which are part of self-preservation. It is right that we control them and are conscious of their potential corrosive influence. But a sense of agitation or anger can be a powerful stimulus for good, in the sense of generating the determination to make change happen.

26 WATCH YOUR FRIENDSHIPS

Be loyal, but not in a blinkered way

Mutual trust and a sense of shared endeavour are important for many of us. We like to work with people we like. It is much easier to build a successful partnership with people with whom there is a strong sense of common purpose, shared effort and mutual support. We relish working with colleagues with whom there is a warmth of relationship.

But when are these emotional bonds a positive help and when can they be a hindrance? How much is personal loyalty a strength or a liability? When can the strength of professional friendship undermine the effectiveness of a working relationship?

❖ John's story:

John thoroughly enjoyed working in the same hospital as David and Ben as they were an excellent team. They had helped each other out on numerous occasions, and John knew he could rely on David and Ben for their support and encouragement.

But Ben had become tired and less effective. David and John tried to understand what had happened to Ben's confidence. They were determined to support and encourage him, but the problems became more acute. John and David talked about what friendship meant in this situation. They recognised that good friendship meant saying to Ben that he needed to move to a different sphere in order to rekindle his energy and enthusiasm. Friendship for John and David was about loyalty and support, but not in such a way that the work of the hospital suffered. The patients came first and not their friendship with Ben.

For many of us one of the main enjoyments of work comes from the interchange with good colleagues. The exchanges of ideas and practical suggestions help ignite our enthusiasm. Working with good colleagues develops our confidence and competence. The building of professional relationships is akin to friendship in terms of mutual understanding, rapport and encouragement.

Effective dialogue with colleagues, clients and customers depends on the building of trust and empathy. Effective networking is all about building relationships where there is a mutuality of interest. Good professional relationships and networking are about more than self-interest. Part of our own personal fulfilment comes from the quality of engagement we have with other people. Engagement that is creative and leads to practical results builds a sense of mutual respect, commitment and loyalty.

Mutual loyalty is essential for any team or group to work together well. Formal contractual arrangements create a structured mutuality, but in most cases, the quality of interaction is not based on the dry words of a contract. It results from warmth and a sense of co-operation. We often feel at our best when we sense the encouragement and support of others.

But loyalty can be dangerous. Good appointments are about appointing the most suitable person to do a particular job. Appointments based on friendship will be seen to be nepotistic and not in the best interests of the organisation. But it is entirely natural for any interviewing panel to be saying to themselves, "Which of the candidates am I happiest to be spending time with?" Personal chemistry is essential for any group of people to work well together and cannot be ignored. But where there is a preference to work with someone with whom you have worked with before, that can be a dangerous expression of personal loyalty.

Too much loyalty can get in the way of creating a successful business, school, hospital or university building, diversity and fairness to all the potential candidates trump personal loyalty. Personal loyalty can get in the way of giving someone hard messages. Every working relationship has a lifespan. There will always be a terminus when working relationships need to change and we need to move on. Recognising when professional working relationships need to change and move into a different space is a tough recognition of reality that is essential and can be painful. It can be important for a good, professional friend to say it is time for you to move on.

Practical steps

Some practical points of reflection might be:

- What are the professional friendships you treasure most and why?
- What are the professional relationships you want to cultivate even more?
- When have you become too close and loyal to someone?

If you reflect on a particular working relationship that is akin to a friendship:

- Are there risks that it is too cosy?
- Is there an extent to which the friendship means you are blinded to the limitations of your colleague?
- How best might that working relationship move to the next level of effectiveness?

Good friendship is precious, we want to embrace it and hold on to it. And yet the best professional friendships are evolving all the time. Good working relationships need regular review or they become stuck and uncreative. Treasuring the dynamic nature of friendships in a working environment is precious, while recognising that emotional bonds can sometimes become obsessive and counter-productive.

BUILD YOUR APPROACH

It is difficult to stand still for a long time. When I was a member of the Combined Cadet Force at school we were told to bend our knees or rock back on our heels in order to avoid the risk of stiffening up or keeling over. But inevitably during a long parade some would faint. It is easier, physically, to keep moving forward than to stand still for a long period.

In a leadership role it is difficult to be static for long. You are either moving forward with energy and commitment, or falling backwards if the enthusiasm and energy is sapped and work activity becomes dull and does not engage you.

This section is about continually building your approach so you keep moving forward and reduce the risk of going backwards. Using analogies from gardening it covers "cultivating your carrots", "pruning the rose trees", "nurturing the green shoots" and "enjoying the bonfire". The Chinese have an expression: "If you want to be happy for a week, get married. If you wish to be happy for a month, slaughter a pig. If you wish to be happy for ever, plant a garden." A garden needs constant vigilance and work if the plants are to grow and not wither.

27 CULTIVATE YOUR CARROTS

Treasure your eyesight

When carrots are growing there is a healthy, green plant on the surface but the interesting activity is below ground where they are full of life and flourishing. We often need to present a healthy and attractive-looking demeanour to the wider world, but the activity that is most important is whether, down below, we are growing in strength and insight. What matters for the long term is often hidden from view. Brought into the sunlight too quickly, the baby carrot shrivels up when it would have been best left in the ground for much longer.

When she was a student, my wife Frances worked at a vegetable laboratory. One of its remits was to cultivate a strain of carrot that would grow to a consistent size and shape, and therefore be easier to put in cans than carrots of more varied shapes and sizes. Standardising the product was commercially sensible in order to get as many carrots as possible into a can. But carrots out of cans are often bland in taste. Standardisation helps commercially, but taking out the variety means the product becomes less appealing. If an organisation tries to mould all their leaders into the same shape, that may be fine up to a point but like canned carrots, they may become bland and tasteless.

We can easily judge carrots by their appearance. Supermarkets sell carrots that are perfectly shaped as top quality products. Those that are misshapen are lumped together and sold at a discount price. I always buy the most misshapen carrots which often seem to have more taste and character. The perfectly shaped and scrubbed carrot is somehow not as appealing as the carrot that has recently come out of the ground and looks to have a bit of character.

It is possible to reflect on the analogy of the carrot when we think about leaders and managers we admire. They are rarely bland and shaped the same way. They are unlikely to have been scrubbed perfectly clean. They are more likely to be individual in shape, earthy in character, able to catch the imagination and are appealing to those watching.

Carrots require nurturing. They need plenty of water and space to grow. They are dependent upon nutrients in the ground so that they can expand and become strong and healthy. When we want to develop a new approach or become better at handling a situation it can take time for this approach or 'carrot' to grow. It will need nurturing, watering and developing, and will be hidden from view initially, before it becomes distinctive and full of quality and flavour.

❖ Geoff's story:

Geoff felt nervous whenever he had to give presentations to a big group. Inwardly he shrivelled up and did not like the exposure. He knew he needed to develop this competence. He defined two or three ways in which he needed to build his confidence and expertise. He practised giving presentations on subjects he knew well to small audiences. These were modest occasions, hidden from view but the encouragement and good feedback he received gave him the confidence to keep developing his presentation skills. He now felt stronger which showed in his voice and outward demeanour. There was no sense of shrivelling up. When the time for a big presentation came he felt different, he sounded more assured and his audience were more convinced.

Practical steps

Is there an approach you need to cultivate and grow? Perhaps it is about giving presentations, influencing large groups, having challenging conversations or giving unwelcome feedback well. If there is an approach you want to develop, practical steps might include:

• Define objectively and unemotionally what is the approach you want to grow and what success would look like
• Define the two or three areas where you need to be clear on your approach and practise these approaches
• Create or use situations which are not high profile where you can try out and experiment with your preferred approach
• Keep reviewing your progress and deciding on next steps

The metaphor of cultivating your carrots has many dimensions to it. Might you reflect on what aspects of the metaphor amuse you and are relevant to how you grow your contribution in your work?

28 PRUNE YOUR APPLE TREES

Cut back to grow forward

We have a couple of apple trees in our garden which produce colourful blossom. When we cut the trees back they look bare, lonely and bedraggled, but they grow again and look even healthier than before. The glorious blossom is followed by good crops of apples. If we did not cut the trees back they would not produce such wonderful blossom and apples.

The idea of cutting back the branches seems destructive. Are we not damaging the tree? Will it ever grow again? And yet it is as if the tree wants to be pruned. The best quality apples only come after the trees have been cut back.

It feels fine to be cutting out dead wood. Removing dead branches does not cause a problem. It is when we cut back branches that are alive that we question whether it is prudent to do so. What matters is the recognition that there is a cycle of growth, then cutting back, going through a period of apparent barrenness and then enjoying the bursting blossom and fruit that is full of flavour.

If the apple tree is not pruned it will become big and ungainly. Pruning back the branches means that the apple tree keeps its shape, its fruit can be reached and it does not get entwined with other apple trees growing in the same area. Pruning means it looks less bedraggled and chaotic so its fruit can be harvested easily and successfully. The apple tree thrives because it is pruned. It may not be an attractive process and is certainly not pain-free for the apple tree but it thrives, blossoms, grows and bears quality fruits because it is pruned.

Sometimes we try new approaches that do not work. We build new working relationships that are not productive. We spend time on projects that lead nowhere. A periodic pruning session may be exactly what we need. We may need to reduce the time and energy that goes into particular activities. We may conclude that a particular working relationship is going nowhere. A creative enterprise we have begun may have no market. Robust pruning can be desirable, if painful.

When we have pruned back to the bare necessities and are focusing on the essentials, life may seem a bit dull and exposed. But once pruned, there is more opportunity for new life. After a period when we appear to get no benefit from the pruning, we can blossom in new ways and bear more productive fruit than before.

❖ Francois' story:

Francois was permanently busy. As a marketing manager he had developed a whole sequence of projects. Some were productive and bearing fruit while others seemed to be active enough but with no apparent results. All the projects Francois had initiated were worthwhile, but the combined effect was sapping energy and meaning such that there was little coherence about the direction of his organisation.

Francois knew he needed to get the pruning shears out. One or two projects were easily stopped because there was little life in them. Other projects, although still energetic, needed to be stopped for the good of the whole organisation so they could focus on the projects likely to have the most impact. Francois pruned hard and was not always welcomed. But the pruning was essential and after a painful period Francois' organisation became more coherent. Staff and clients knew where it was going and what it stood for.

Practical steps

Can you stand back from the range of activities you are involved in? Are there activities that need pruning? Questions to ask might include:

- What activities are sapping energy and being less productive than other activities?
- What working relationships are going nowhere?
- What elements of your time are least productive?
- What are the dead branches you could easily remove?
- What are the branches that are alive but less productive?

Pruning living branches is never easy. Helpful questions might be:

- What might grow in its place if this branch is cut off?
- What benefit does the whole tree receive because some branches are pruned?
- What is the blossom I want to see grow that I can keep in my mind's eye when I do the pruning?

29 NURTURE THE GREEN SHOOTS

Talk to the saplings

I remember as a child planting cress seeds in a pot and watching expectedly for the green shoots to appear. I remember the excitement as the green shoots forced their way through. When reseeding an area of lawn nothing seems to happen for a while, and then there is a thin haze of green when the first seeds have germinated and the fine green leaves of grass begin to appear.

We can soon kill off green shoots by walking on the lawn before the grass is strong or dense enough to cope. We can assume the grass is strong and robust long before it has spread itself enough to become hardy. We can underestimate the time that the green shoots need to grow into full strength and maturity.

Green shoots appear in unexpected places. Sometimes they need nurturing. On other occasions, they grow of their own accord. Often they are mixed in with weeds and other unwelcome plants. Looking after green shoots well means watering and tending them, as well as removing the weeds and other plants that stifle their growth.

Sometimes the green shoots are doing so well that they need to be replanted. They need to go from the nursery bed into a more permanent location. The movement from one bed to another can be disruptive, hence the care needed in replanting. Sometimes the growth in the green shoots is so dense that they need to be thinned, with the shoots that are growing less strongly given more space or removed.

Green shoots search for the light. They bend to ensure that they get maximum exposure to the sun. But they are also pushed around by the wind and may not have the strength to cope with a storm. Sometimes the green shoots will need sheltering under a canopy, but to become fully hardy they will need exposure to whatever the weather has to offer.

Green shoots have a simplicity and freshness that is attractive. They can be a delight to the eye and an encouragement that new life is part of the cycle of nature, but green shoots are fragile and need care and attention. Not all will survive and grow into full maturity.

The metaphor of the green shoots can be about observing the green shoots in ourselves. What are the new ideas which need nurturing and looking after? What thoughts about the future are gradually growing: how can we help them come to fruition? What are the green shoots we see in other people which we can encourage and nurture?

Are we at risk of trampling on the green shoots in ourselves and others and not allowing them to grow to fruition? Can we stand back more and enjoy the green shoots and not try and rush them before their time into full maturity?

❖ Joel's story:

Joel enjoyed working with his 15-year-old students. They were often sullen, boorish and uncommunicative. Life seemed to revolve around music, the mobile phone and the internet. But there were always green shoots. Virtually all his students had subjects or activities about which they were enthusiastic. Within the boorish behaviour there were green shoots of energy and aspiration. Joel knew that he needed to cultivate those green shoots, not only because of the merit of the individual interests, but also because it was through these green shoots that these young people were growing into adulthood. The green shoots would, in due course, become sturdy plants in the future.

Practical steps

Might it be helpful to reflect on:

- What are the green shoots in you that are worth recognising, reflecting on and nurturing?
- What are the green shoots in others you want to recognise, encourage and develop?

Over the next couple of weeks, might you identify:

- One green shoot in yourself you want to cultivate?
- One green shoot in another person to whom you are willing to commit time to enable them to recognise the green shoot and to enable it to grow in them?

30 ENJOY THE BONFIRE

Be warmed by the glow

There is something satisfying about watching the glow of a bonfire. The combination of the warmth, the dancing flames and burning embers draws us to the bonfire. A bonfire might have been hard work to build, but there is a special pleasure about watching the activity within the bonfire.

In the autumn it can be quite satisfying accumulating dead branches and fallen leaves and then creating a bonfire. We can be energised by this sense of sorting out, tidying up and making ready for the winter. We have bonfires less often these days with the emphasis on recycling, which sees the leaves composted, the branches in the wood burning stove and cardboard recycled, as we want to create as little waste as possible.

The metaphor of the bonfire is about removing waste and the irrelevant, heaping it up and setting it alight. The enjoyment comes through watching the glow as we see what is no longer relevant or useful going up in flames.

But the emphasis on recycling and not wasting is relevant too. What are the gifts and abilities we can reuse in different ways? What might previously have been regarded as irrelevant that we can now use in a different way? Perhaps an underused gift of writing can be reused in a different way rather than left to waste. Sometimes we want to throw things into the bonfire when we could use that knowledge or skill with different people in other contexts rather than discard it.

We do need to be mindful that the language of throwing things into the bonfire can appear arrogant. Governments can talk about having a bonfire of particular organisations and not appear to have any regard for the individual commitment that has gone into making those organisations work well. The language of the bonfire can appear destructive and disrespectful, however necessary a change in an organisation might be.

History is littered with destructive bonfires where political or religious causes have led to the burning of books written by people of whom they disapprove. Such provocative events remind us that bonfires can be symbols of hatred. Hence the importance of clarity about reasons for bonfires. It is not just about enjoying the glow of the embers, it is being clear that the bonfire is there to enable new life and activity to be created and is not there to destroy values and purpose that are the bedrock of the communities in which we live and work.

❖ Barbara's story:

Barbara felt stuck. She was a health and safety inspector who was passionate about her work but felt continually pushed back by the people she worked with who did not seem to appreciate her contribution. Her day was cluttered with a wide range of different activities, some of which were more relevant and useful than others. Her mind was full of both positive steps she wanted to take forward in her role, but also frustrations and resentment which kept circling around her mind. Barbara loved having bonfires in her garden. Perhaps she needed a bonfire in her head.

Barbara knew that she needed to crystallise her priorities more clearly. She needed to rid herself of the attitudes that were destructive, especially the resentment that was contaminating everything else. Barbara used the image of the bonfire to rid herself of some of the tasks that were less important and the attitudes that were destructive. She enjoyed the glow and felt able to move on, less inhibited by the noise in her head, and more focused on where she could contribute in her work.

Practical steps

If you were to have a bonfire in a week's time, what might you throw on the bonfire? Might the bonfire involve:

- Discarding certain ways of doing things that are now outdated?
- Removing some activities that have ceased to be priorities?
- Boxing and burning some frustrations that you want to move on from?
- Casting some resentments deep into the flames?

Can you let the mental picture of a bonfire allow you to:

- Get rid of some approaches and attitudes?
- Leave space for new priorities?
- Be warmed by the glow?

USE YOUR TIME WELL

Time is one of the most precious commodities we have. We want to make the most productive use of our time but sometimes we need to go slow to go fast. On other occasions we need to operate quickly and without hesitation.

Sometimes we can allocate time for a particular activity. On other occasions time is used up by other people and there is a high degree of unpredictability about what is possible in any given period. New technology is a practical help to using time well, but can also be a hindrance when it focuses us on short-term results and not long-term reflection or strategy.

This section focuses on different aspects of using time well, including: "walk ever so slowly" which is about pacing down; "ditch the Blackberry" which is about using new technology well; "adjusting your personal rhythms" which is about the use of cycles in time management that works well for you; and "balancing the see-saw" which is about balancing different priorities.

31 WALK EVER SO SLOWLY

Go slow to go fast

When hiking over difficult terrain you have to go slow to go fast. If the ground is slippery rushing only leads to slipping and twisted ankles. When the terrain is rough it is purposeful footsteps at a measured pace which ensures steady progress. If the terrain is icy progress demands slow, measured footsteps with regular reassessment of the degree of slipperiness and stability.

If a problem is complicated rushing to a solution might seem the easy way, but not necessarily the best way. What might be needed is testing a proposition, but in a way that looks at the potential solution from different angles and tests its robustness. The best approach might be to go slow to go fast, chunking up a task into manageable steps and then taking on each one carefully, in a purposeful way.

❖ Felix's story:

Felix had a difficult problem to solve in setting the timetable at his sixth form college. There were many different constraints and preferences. Lots of people wanted to "advise" him. He had various computer programmes to help him.

Felix knew that his final proposal would be tested against both professional and personal priorities. He had inherited a system that felt random and shambolic. He was determined to build a timetable that had broad acceptance. Felix went slowly at first, talking to lots of different people while building a clear picture of preferences and priorities. He tested out different permutations and relied on those he trusted to look through his first proposals. His final proposition built on shared agreements and was broadly accepted. Felix had gained some allies who were willing to support his proposals strongly. He had gone slowly, step by step, and reached a good outcome.

However important the task and whatever the time scale required of us, it can be broken down into steps. Everest was climbed one step at a time. Each task can be broken down into manageable elements.

Speed may be imposed by others or by our own perspective about what success is. We often want to impress and to get to a point of conclusion quickly. We can become nervous if we are not making the progress which we judge to be necessary. But a hurried exercise can become a botched job. A piece of major engineering which contains one technical inaccuracy can be fatally flawed.

But sometimes speed is essential. A crisis needs to be addressed. But even a crisis will include different steps of response with measured communication an essential element. Listening to people working in an emergency services call centre makes you realise how important measured calmness is when taking a call from a distraught person who is seeking an ambulance. Often, the phone operator would deliberately speak slowly to extract the key information needed to send the ambulance to the right place.

The barrister may want to put a witness under pressure to elicit information. But part of the successful barrister's repertoire is the ability to slow the questioning down so that the witness is forced to keep going more deeply into his recollection of a particular incident. A good journalist knows to ask tough questions but also leaves plenty of space for the interviewee to set out his views more fully, and potentially give the journalist some phrases which the interviewee had not initially intended to use.

When a dialogue is not going the way you want, sometimes it is right to be assertive and push back. On other occasions the most appropriate technique might be to allow someone to keep talking and consequently overstate their argument, giving you the opportunity to draw out the downsides of their approach.

Practical steps

Some practical steps about slowing down in order to go fast might be:

- See each task as a sequence of steps
- Accept that a significant investment of time in preparation and in groundwork is always going to pay dividends
- Be ready to recognise the progress you have made when it has been made, one step at a time

If you are part of a major activity which you think would benefit from being taken forward a bit more slowly, might you:

- Encourage others to review the timetable
- Be clear what are the key factors that need to be sorted before progress can be made
- Build alliances with others about the most important issues to be addressed first

Walking ever so slowly is not about laziness. It can be about recognising that you are in for the long haul. Using all your energy and creativity in the first few moves may mean you are building on a thin foundation. Effective preparation both individually and with others as you move a step at a time is rarely wasted.

32

DITCH THE BLACKBERRY

Do I have to carry my Blackberry on my back?

We would look very foolish if we went around carrying an in-tray on our back. We would laugh if someone was walking round with their in-tray with a foot of papers strapped to their back. We would assume they were being conscientious but inept. We would be at risk of not taking them seriously.

And yet we admire someone who carries a Blackberry and always looks as if they are in control. A Blackberry has become a symbol of being up to date and treating people responsibly by responding quickly to their every wish. But is this always the best use of our time?

❖ Mary's story:

Mary used her Blackberry to keep up to date with her email. She prided herself on being available to her colleagues. But sometimes she wanted to throw the Blackberry across the room. It was relentless. It was permanently bleeping. No one was willing to leave her alone. Because she responded quickly, people expected her to respond quickly so all her efficiency did was generate ever higher expectations from other people.

One day, Mary left her Blackberry at home. Strangely, she got a lot of work done that day without the regular disturbance of the Blackberry. She completed some tasks that she had previously not had the mental space to deal with. She got home elated because of the progress made and resisted the temptation to look at the Blackberry until the following morning.

The availability of emails and texts on handheld machines has radically changed the way we communicate. It is a beneficial change in many ways. We can always be in touch and be kept up to date. We no longer have the problem of travelling some distance to a meeting only to find that it has been cancelled with our not having been able to be informed in advance.

But instant communication tends to require instant response. A minor suggestion can produce a flurry of emails or text messages. Was it necessary to spend all that energy commenting on one small issue?

Sometimes we send an email when a short conversation on the phone would be more appropriate. Some organisations have experimented with email-free days to put the focus back on face-to-face communication. Individuals have felt liberated by the focus on conversation rather than electronic communication.

It can be a refreshing exercise to reflect on how you would communicate with key individuals if the Blackberry was not available and then deliberately using this effective form of communication. Electronic communication has become our initial form of contact when it may be more appropriate as a last resort.

What sometimes helps is clear contracting between individuals about the sort of interaction they are happy to have electronically and when oral communication becomes important. Electronic communication can create fixed, rigid views with no flexibility to develop arguments or approaches. Using the PC or Blackberry in a focused way can help chunk up the day and be an efficient use of time, but the compulsive use of technology or being impulsive in responding are dangers that can so easily be fallen into.

What would happen if you did not look at your Blackberry for a day or even a week? If someone wanted to get in contact with you urgently they would telephone you. But other than in certain, particular roles do you have to be available 24 hours a day, seven days a week?

Practical steps

Some practical approaches to using electronic communications better
may include:

- Box the amount of time you look at electronic communications
- Be deliberately selective about what form of communication you use on
  different subjects with particular people
- Be active with the 'delete' button and restrained in the use of the 'reply
  all' button
- Give yourself time before replying whenever the subject is sensitive

If you feel addicted to the Blackberry, can you experiment with:

- Only turning the Blackberry on once a day
- Not taking it with you on holiday or restricting its use to occasional
  purposes
- Becoming increasingly selective about when you communicate
  electronically and when orally

We can feel burdened by communication. When we leave the
Blackberry behind can we imagine it is like leaving a heavy rucksack on
the ground? When we pick up the Blackberry again, can we train ourselves
to do so in a way that it is disciplined and restrained in its use? Can we be
amused by the amount of wasted words that people seem to transmit via
the Blackberry?

33

ADJUST YOUR PERSONAL RHYTHMS

Recognise when you are at your best

Are you a morning person or an evening person? We all are conscious of when we are at our best and when our thinking is at its clearest. Sometimes we are able to spend time and energy in a way that is consistent with our preferences. On other occasions we feel constrained and shoehorn our preferences into the expectations of the organisation within which we work. How do we get the best balance between the rhythms that work well for us and the requirements of our organisation and our colleagues?

The increased use of flexible working and electronic means of communication open up new possibilities in terms of matching our preferences to the needs of the organisation we are working within. Building a rhythm that works for us is not just about selfish preference, it is ensuring that the output we generate is directed in the most effective way to the needs of the organisation that is paying our salary.

❖ Marcia's story:

Marcia struggled about when and where she did her creative thinking. She needed to devise a new syllabus for her pupils. Marcia recognised that she could not do this easily within the school environment. For a few days she left school promptly when the formal day ended and spent a couple of hours each evening for a week developing the syllabus. Setting aside space and time for this purpose at home worked well for Marcia. She knew that for her colleague, Ethel, doing creative thinking at home was not possible because there was too much noise there.

For Ethel, creating a new syllabus in her subject was best done in the school environment after the pupils had left. They both recognised each other's preferences and worked with the grain of those preferences to ensure they were both able to complete their syllabuses. The Head Teacher was ready to encourage Marcia to work at home and Ethel to work at school on their development projects.

The personal rhythms that work for us have developed over time. They can be hereditary, or a result of education and experience or the circumstances in which we find ourselves. But personal rhythm can be modified. Sometimes a new role or a change to the work environment can mean that adjustments to personal rhythm are necessary. We may recognise that with the passage of time a modified approach is needed to deliver our best.

It can be helpful to list the type of activities you are involved in and note for each of them when you are at your best in terms of the time of day, the people you are with, the environment you are in and the amount of pressure you do or do not put yourself under. A crude, arithmetic scoring system about when you are at your best, by time of day or environment, can give a rough ranking about when might be the best time to undertake different activities.

You do not have to be available to everyone all the time. Boxing time for particular purposes can help ensure the variety which brings out the best in you. A day solid with one sort of activity is rarely going to bring out the best in us. But splitting a day into different sorts of activities spent with different people might give us the stimulus we need to do the boring tasks well!

Chunking a day into one-hour blocks can be a valuable discipline, provided not all the blocks are of the same degree of intensity and there is opportunity for a change of gear during the work day. Triathletes have to swim, cycle and run well. They know how to pace themselves for these three very different activities and acknowledge that they will be quicker at one of them than the other two. They know how to use their energy in order to be successful in the overall competition. If they swim too fast they will be exhausted when it comes to the running.

Practical steps

Some practical steps in adjusting your personal rhythms might include:

- Can you block out time which you can use for creative and new thinking?
- Can you identify the time and place when you are best able to handle difficult problems well?
- How best do you maximise the occasions when you are operating at your best?

If you think forward to next week:

- How will you handle the difficult issues you need to solve?
- How will you create some space to do some practical forward thinking?
- How will you ensure you are at your best for the meetings that are most important?
- How will you ensure you do not get exhausted?

We tend to get caught within particular patterns in the way we work and allow others to reinforce previous expectations. It can be helpful to take a radical look and assess whether a more flexible working pattern might allow you to make changes to the rhythm in the way you spend your time and energy. It can be worth experimenting doing different pieces of work in different locations.

34 BALANCE THE SEE-SAW

It would be so dull if it was straightforward

We look forward to times when we have one objective and a clear pathway ahead. But when we hit these ideal moments we can rapidly become bored. We like some degree of variety, although the point at which helpful variety becomes unhelpful distraction will vary from one person to another.

If a new task has got to be done a part of us will want to protest that we are being taken in the wrong direction and away from what is most important, while another part of us will relish the change and the opportunity to have a different stimulus.

How do we best balance the see-saw when we have varied expectations placed upon us, especially when those priorities come from different individuals and may mean a dissonance between professional and personal preferences?

❖ **William's story:**

William worked as a senior member of staff in a prison. The Prison Governor knew that William would be willing to take on whatever responsibilities he gave him. William was keen to build up goodwill from the Governor but recognised that he had a tendency to take on too much. William also knew that he thrived when he had a range of different responsibilities.

William recognised that he needed to live within his own energies and be clear that his boss was not expecting him to do more than was humanly possible. William's agreement with the Prison Governor was that they would take stock every two or three weeks to agree on relative priorities.

This was an essential discipline to ensure that the expectations on William were consistent with what was possible to deliver. William was happy to live slightly on the edge, but needed a clear understanding with his boss that he could vary the time scale about what could be achieved to take into account the changed pressures upon him.

Balancing the see-saw can have a range of different dimensions. Sometimes it is about the balance between leading and managing. The priority one week might be steering and motivating other people, while in another week one might need to be hands-on to ensure a project is executed effectively.

The focus might sometimes be on what you are doing as an individual. On other occasions it might be on what you are doing as part of a team to ensure the overall team delivers effectively. The balance may sometimes be on the short term where immediate tasks have to be completed. On other occasions the focus should probably be on the long term, building a pathway ahead and ensuring that key relationships and strategies are in place.

Another important balance is between activity and reflection. Activity to get things done, whatever the organisation we work in, is necessary for progress to be made. But activity needs to be built on a foundation which is well thought through based on clear analysis and reflection. A further point of balance might be between being resolute and being adaptable. A clear, single-minded approach is often essential but sometimes adaptability is crucial to meet a timetable or to respond to changed circumstances.

We may be balancing certainty and uncertainty. We can have certain fixed points, but have to recognise that some issues are difficult to resolve and we have to live with some lack of clarity. Sometimes ambiguity is not going to be solved. We need to co-exist with people who have different expectations where forcing clarity would be counter-productive. Living with a degree of ambiguity is never straightforward, but may be the only way of ensuring that people of different perspectives can co-exist in reasonable harmony.

It can feel like a see-saw where the balance point keeps moving. At least when we are on a see-saw we are unlikely to fall asleep. Perhaps celebrating variety and uncertainty is important, rather than being daunted by it.

Practical steps

Some practical thoughts on balancing the see-saw might include:

- What type of balancing of different priorities stimulates you and how best do you thrive when balancing such priorities?
- What type of balancing of priorities do you find difficult to handle and how best can you develop greater ease in handling conflicting priorities?
- How best do you live with uncertainty or ambiguity?

Looking ahead to current priorities you face which may be in conflict, what might you do to:

- Agree with other key people what are the main priorities
- How might you explicitly rebalance the priorities in a way which is acceptable to your boss and your colleagues?
- Which of the uncertainties can you leave alone and say to yourself that they can be left unresolved for a period?

Sitting on a see-saw can be great fun. The movement up and down can cause us to laugh and smile. But being on a permanent see-saw can give us a sore bottom and a headache! Riding a see-saw is sometimes what working life is like and learning to smile and laugh at the jolts is part of survival, as is knowing when to get off the see-saw and take a break.

BE ALERT TO THE UNEXPECTED

We learn about the importance of preparation and planning. We like to plan ahead and to know what is coming next. We have experienced the benefits of effective preparation and planning and want to maintain a structured, disciplined approach. We recognise that unpredictability is inevitable, and spend time analysing risks and trying to reduce uncertainties to a minimum.

But the unexpected does happen. We can enjoy the unexpected because it leads to our having new energy. Handling the unexpected can be great fun. We can be surprised by good things while recognising that we can daunted by the unwelcome and unexpected.

This section looks at different aspects of being alert to the unexpected. It covers looking for hidden treasure, not counting your chickens, being wary of false dawns, enjoying shafts of sunlight and knowing where your snowshoes are. My hope is that these thoughts will enable you to relish the prospect of the unexpected rather than be daunted by it.

35 LOOK FOR HIDDEN TREASURE

Be ready to be surprised

As a child, a summer treat was to visit Scarborough Mere in the north of England and go on the pirate ship to a small island. We would be invited to dig in the sand and search for "pieces of silver". It was an exciting adventure I looked forward to. There was a mystery about searching for hidden treasure and wondering what sort of coins I would find. It was, of course, entirely planned and predictable as the "pirates" had buried the pieces of silver in advance. But as a child there was always new excitement about looking for hidden treasure.

Looking for the unexpected can bring a sense of excitement. Searching for new insights in science, engineering or medicine is both professionally and personally absorbing. Looking for a new approach to solve a design problem can revitalise a team which wants to deliver the best possible outcome.

❖ Amanda's story:

Amanda was a research scientist with a pharmaceutical company trying to refine a particular drug. She had tried a range of different approaches to give her the outcome she wanted but none worked. It was like searching for hidden treasure as she tried different permutations. At last, after a number of tests, she felt she was making some progress. What kept her going was this picture of striving for hidden treasure through creating a variant of the drug that would make a big difference for patients.

Treasure can be something tangible or a new insight or understanding. Hidden treasure may be something that is not immediately obvious which might take a long time to discover.

Hidden treasure for a scientist might be a new discovery or a new technique. Hidden treasure for an information technology specialist might be the unexpected bi-product of trying to refine an existing process. Hidden treasure for an engineer might be an insight which helps convert a complicated problem into a simple set of next steps.

When we are working on a particular activity we may not want to be surprised. But allowing ourselves to be surprised by the reactions of different people can give us new insights about the problem, its solution and the reaction of people in similar situations. Being alert to our own surprise and that of others can allow us to look at issues from a variety of different angles and then see a central truth about next steps that had previously been hidden from us.

When we deal with any problem, if we believe that there is a solution which might be currently hidden from view, we are more likely to keep up the resolve to solve the problem. "The treasure is there but is hidden" is likely to be a much more effective mantra than "I cannot see what is supposed to be the treasure ahead".

Looking for hidden treasure is about searching in different places for insights and new information. It is allowing our imagination to take us to different viewpoints so our eyes can search out what had previously been obscured from view. If our approach is that there are always new angles to be discovered, then we are much more likely to keep fresh and alert to new and exciting possibilities.

Practical steps

Some practical ways of enhancing your ability to see hidden treasure might include:

- Believing that treasure is there to be found
- Re-defining 'hidden' as not quite visible yet
- Looking forward to being surprised

Over the next few weeks looking for hidden treasure might include:

- Enjoying the unexpected
- Looking at problems from a range of different perspectives
- Allowing yourself the touch of excitement that you might find hidden treasure within new insights

Treasure comes in different shapes and sizes. It can be new methods, new information, new insights or new ways of working. Looking for treasure and then treasuring what we discover is part of thriving in our work even when life is busy and relentless.

36 DON'T COUNT YOUR CHICKENS

You cross the finishing line when you cross the finishing line

His proud parents were watching Johnnie lead the 400 metres run at his school. He looked way ahead and visibly began to relax. Unfortunately, Andrew was gradually catching up on Johnnie and overtook him with a few metres to go. Johnnie was desolate. He thought he had already won the race. He was so confident of success that he had slowed down.

Johnnie's parents knew that they had to stand with Johnnie and cheer him up. There was no need to tell Johnnie that he had learned a lesson. He was not going to make that mistake again. He would now keep going until he crossed the finishing line, rather than slowing down in advance.

It helps to be confident that we can reach our destination. We need to be able to pace our energies and not feel desperate to cross the finishing line. But we can never assume that we will reach our destination or that everything will work out just as we had hoped.

As soon as we assume success is guaranteed we might begin to lose focus and energy. Our brain can become less attuned to receiving information. Our emotions may become insensitive to the concerns or doubts of those around us. A sense of strong focused endeavour can turn into a more disparate wandering without focus and energy, slipping into a lower gear.

❖ Carole's story:

Carole had been leading a project with a tight deadline and had managed the process superbly. The confidence within her had been a positive contributor to success as her approach was that every problem could be solved. But the confidence sometimes meant she did everything herself as others lacked the initiative to get things done within the agreed framework. A few days before the deadline she was so confident of success that she became embroiled in other work issues and had a busy social diary. She missed some warning signs that all was not well and was shocked when her staff said the deadline would not be met. This warning meant that on future occasions she used her time and energy in a more focused way enabling others to do a lot of the detailed work while she focused on addressing key risks.

We often face the dilemma of having to make assumptions without guaranteed evidence. We have to assume that others will be able to deliver their contributions on time and at the expected quality. We cannot assume that it will always happen, but we can minimise the risks by how we select and train people for particular roles and provide appropriate mentoring and oversight.

Leaving "rattle space" can be so important in providing an opportunity to catch up if a contribution is delayed. "Just in time" is a proven way of doing things in manufacturing. But it is a risky way of getting teams to work well. Most of us need space to assess whether our preparations are working, whether the context has changed and how our contribution is going to be received. "Not counting your chickens" is about keeping up the resolve right to the end, but it is also about having some capacity to check, review and reposition so that we do meet the right deadline at the right place, at the right time.

Practical steps

Some practical ways of ensuring that you do not become over confident and "count your chickens" too early can include:

- Be clear about the progress you are making towards a particular milestone and always be realistic about what has been delivered and what is still to be done
- Watch when you might be at risk of becoming over confident and losing some focus and energy
- Be conscious of the pattern of when you prepare most effectively, what distracts you and when you are at risk of making assumptions that are too optimistic
- Recognise when your confidence is a powerful, positive influence, and when it can tip into an over confidence that results in complacency

Over the next few weeks being careful not to "count your chickens" too soon might involve:

- Assessing whether your confidence that a particular project will be delivered is rooted in fact or fantasy
- Ensuring that you have enough "rattle space" within different activities so there is time to modify your approach if it is not working effectively

37   BEWARE OF FALSE DAWNS

When others indulge your optimism too much

We like to be encouraged and told that all is going well. We need affirmation to keep up our morale. We are told that we should keep giving people good feedback: we want to encourage them and enable them to become ever more effective.

But can we sometimes slip into being overly optimistic which leads people to think they are making progress when little has been made? When I tried to learn to play the piano at the age of 10, my teacher was an encourager, but after a while it felt unconvincing as I knew I was making no progress. She kept saying I was doing well, when I knew I wasn't. Did I collude with her over optimism or recognise the truth of my lack of musical ability or application? Eventually I stopped going to piano lessons.

False dawns can limit our aspirations. We are sceptical about them, do not take them seriously, and therefore may not build effectively on the opportunities that are available to us.

❖ Ann's story:

Ann was told by her boss that she was superb at writing reports. She therefore kept writing them in the same way, whatever the subject. The glowing feedback led her to believe that there was only one way to write a report. Her approach became rigid and inflexible. When challenged to write them differently, Ann insisted that hers was by far the best way to do it. Ann did not want to change her approach, even though the reports were read with less and less enthusiasm.

Part way through an activity a glimmer of light and a word of encouragement is very important. But often the most effective words are about recognition of progress made, bringing new insights, and moving the issue forward, rather than bland words of encouragement. Encouragement that leads to complacency is counter productive. But if they lead to a renewed energy or an adapted focus, then those words of encouragement can be very powerful.

The dawn is about the awakening of a new day. The dawn is the start of the next phase and not the end of the journey. We can be in danger of wanting to find a solution quickly and then clutching to what seems like the right answer. When there are new insights or perspectives early in a process, they provide a starting point for investigation and reflection, and not the end of the journey.

At dawn the light is dim with different facets of the landscape not yet being highlighted. We can freeze in our mind a sight at dawn then we should let the picture evolve over the day with the light coming from different directions which will highlight different features of the landscape and allow us to see an issue from a variety of angles. The dawn is a special time, but the day has many hours to run.

Practical steps

Some practical ways of being aware of false dawns might be:

- When in the past have you experienced a false dawn and what did you learn from that experience?
- When dawn breaks, do you want to stay in that early morning space, or are you open to enjoy different times of the day?
- Can you see different issues, stages of negotiation or portions of work as having a dawn phase, a midday stage and a sun-setting phase? Does that help put different phases and moods into perspective?

Over the next few weeks might you be conscious of:

- What types of dawns are you looking for?
- When you have a new insight, how do you ensure it is not frozen at dawn and is allowed to grow and develop in the sunlight?
- When might there be a risk of over confidence and a false dawn?

False dawns can have a beneficial effect and help us believe there can be progress. But they can also deflate us if what we believe to be true turns out to be unreal. If we did not try out new approaches and risk having false dawns, we would never make progress.

38

WHERE ARE YOUR SNOW SHOES?

Am I ready for the unexpected?

On a wall in our porch are a pair of snow shoes which belonged to my wife's father. They hang above the coat hooks along with a couple of hockey sticks. They are there for decoration rather than use. My father-in-law had used them on a few occasions, but they were a curiosity rather than a necessity.

In some climates snow shoes are a necessity rather than a wise precaution. Knowing whether we need snow shoes flows from our assessment of the risks we face and how best we prepare for them. There is no point in having snow shoes in the Sahara Desert but they might be useful when living in the Arctic Circle.

❖ Zilla's story:

Zilla was a manager who always knew the answer. She knew where the supplies of paper and staples were to be found and who to contact to sort out the photocopier, the door locks and the IT system. There was a risk that colleagues dumped problems on her because she always seemed to know how to find a practical solution. She sometimes felt she was unimportant, but in reality she was one of the most valuable people in the office. She kept the place moving by knowing where everything was and how to sort out practical problems. Hers was a precious contribution to the success of the organisation.

Knowing where your snow shoes are is about knowing how to get out of problematic situations. It is knowing when to walk away and forget, and when to dig in and sort an issue out. Knowing where your snow shoes are is about the practical resources you draw on to handle a range of situations well. It may be about how to get at key data, whose views to seek and where you go for creative insights and how to handle different types of situations.

Snow shoes are designed to be used where there is a lot of snow. In deep snow running shoes are of little use. Knowing the right footwear for the right situation means we do not waste time dragging ourselves around in the wrong footwear. The parallel is about choosing how we walk into different situations and what protection we give our feet. Using our energy well depends on the right kind of footwear for the particular terrain.

In some situations we make our best contribution by listening, contributing little and making key points at the right time. On other occasions, it is right to walk briskly into a situation and make an impact at the start.

It helps if we can be comfortable wearing mountain boots, trainers or snow shoes so that we can respond in an appropriate way in different contexts. Snow shoes are only appropriate in some situations. If we try to wear snow shoes when climbing a mountain we will not get very far, very quickly, especially on a warm summer's day.

Snow shoes might be absolutely the right attire one day and be completely wrong on another occasion when wearing them will mean we grind to a standstill.

If a deep fall of snow is expected there is no point having the snow shoes in the garage roof at the end of the garden. They need to be near the front door so that after heavy snow they can be used. If we want to be able to use our snow shoes, they have got to be accessible.

If we want to use a range of ways to contribute, influence or persuade, we need to know the relevant techniques and be comfortable using them.

If snow shoes are not looked after and are left in the damp, they will disintegrate and become useless. Whatever the approaches we adopt to handle difficult situations well, we need to keep our resources ready for use or they will become less effective and useless.

Practical points

Some ways of thinking about what your snow shoes are might include:

- How willing are you to vary your approach or footwear to meet the different situations?
- How best do you enable yourself to cope in different situations?
- What approaches do you keep ready in case they are needed?

Over the next few weeks:

- When might you need the availability of top quality snow shoes?
- How readily do you switch from one sort of protection for your feet to another?
- How do you ensure that the different approaches that work for you, remain fresh and alive?

Knowing where your snow shoes are is about being prepared in a way that is flexible and matches particular situations with the most appropriate way of handling them.

39 ENJOY SHAFTS OF SUNLIGHT

Don't rush for the shade

When we were in Australia visiting the Grampian mountains we arrived at cricket pitch in a delightful setting. As we reached the cricket field there was a shaft of sunlight between the clouds and we saw loafing about on the cricket field 35 kangaroos enjoying this burst of sunlight. When we went up to them and eyeballed the kangaroos, they eyeballed us back and then kept on grazing.

Shafts of sunlight brighten our day, bring clarity to a grey scene and lift our spirits. A shaft of sunlight in a work context can be a new insight or new perspective which brings an issue to life. A shaft of sunlight can bring a new brightness. What was dull shines, what was grey glitters, what looked tired has new life.

❖ Simon's story:

Simon had been wrestling with a research project for a long time. He had collected a huge amount of data but had not seen a way forward. He tried to analyse the data in different ways but never seemed to reach a clear conclusion. A colleague suggested that he might analyse the data in a different way. Simon was amazed by the correlation in the data this method produced. It was as if a beam of light had been focused on his data and he could see how it all fitted together. Yes – there was a pattern and he could write up his conclusions demonstrating the value of his results. It was as if a shaft of sunlight had helped him see a clear pattern and led him to his conclusions.

Shafts of sunlight are so important. In the winter we can ache for the sun and when the sun shines, our spirits are lifted and we feel much more positive about the world.

We can rush to places where we know we will "get" the sun, but perhaps the most influential shafts of sunlight are those we experience by surprise; they are even more uplifting because they were unplanned.

Shafts of sunlight can be ideas or creative thoughts where we see patterns or opportunities. We need to be open to getting the benefit of shafts of light. That might mean going into the open where we may be more exposed, but more likely to receive shafts of light or insight.

When there is a shaft of light the benefit does not come from looking up at the sun, it comes from looking at what the shaft of light is revealing. We may briefly enjoy looking at the shaft of light, but it is what the light picks out and highlights that matters. To get the full benefit of the sun, we need to look away from the sun. To get the full benefit of a creative thought or insight, we should not dwell on that insight, but see what its impact or influence can be in solving a problem or making a relationship work better to identify the next steps towards solving a problem.

Practical steps
Some practical ways of enjoying shafts of sunlight more might include:
- Be in open places where shafts of sunlight can penetrate
- Look for shafts of sunlight, new perspectives and new insights and do not be fearful about what they might expose
- Search for shafts of sunlight by talking to people who might have new ideas or approaches

Over the next few weeks can you let your imagination play with the following ideas:
- What shafts of sunlight am I looking for?
- Would I recognise a shaft of sunlight or a new insight when I see it?

- How much do I want shafts of sunlight to expose what is hidden?

There is a danger that we are apprehensive about new ideas and perspectives, even though we enjoy a shaft of sunlight on a grey day. Getting ourselves in a frame of mind where we are looking for shafts of sunlight in our working lives can enable us to feel a glow and warmth when new ideas hit us, rather than being fearful of them.

BEWARE THE RISKS

Looking carefully at risks is not a sign of weakness. A robust assessment of risk is central to the success of any venture. Risks can relate to an organisation, the team or an individual. We focus in this section on risks that an individual might face that can throw you off course. Part of thriving is being conscious of what risks might be heading your way and preparing for a range of possibilities. Some risks are almost inevitable and can be planned for, up to a point.

This section addresses four types of risks which can be planned for, at least in terms of emotional readiness! It addresses watching for sharp elbows, being cautious about bright lights, watching for the unexpected and welcoming the health check.

Some of the principles about dealing with these risks are readily transferable to a wider range of risks which we might face. As you reflect on these four risks, there may be others which you want to consider and prepare for.

40 WATCH FOR SHARP ELBOWS

They may be nice to your face, but…

Sometimes the only response when you have been sharp-elbowed is to reflect on the vagaries of human nature. A colleague may be welcoming and friendly one moment, but you might feel their elbow in your ribs shortly thereafter. We may think it is obvious when someone appears to take advantage of us. We may not be so conscious of when we appear to others to have pushed in and used "sharp elbows".

When we observe someone pushing in and taking advantage of a situation, we know what is important to them at that moment. We then have the choice of whether we respond like with like and get our shoulder ready for action, or whether we respond in a deliberately different way.

❖ Carolyn's story:

Carolyn thought she had built up a good relationship with a colleague. They were due to give a joint presentation to the senior leadership team about a new insurance product they had been putting together. Carolyn had trusted her colleague during the process of putting the product together and assumed that that same mutuality would apply in the presentation.

To her surprise, her colleague implied in the presentation that it was his idea and he had taken the lead. Carolyn thought his approach was grossly unfair and decided not to push back immediately after the presentation. But she made sure in a subsequent discussion that she expressed her views clearly and directly. She was determined not to be seen to be in the shadow of her colleague, while at the same time refraining from any overt criticism of her colleague. She responded to the sharp elbows by being firm about her contribution, but not in a way that appeared antagonistic.

Carolyn's colleague may well have been unaware of the impression he had created with Carolyn. He was determined to do well in front of the senior leadership team and either deliberately or inadvertently put himself in the lead position. Often when we feel undermined by someone they are not doing it intentionally. In the heat of the moment the natural, human instinct of wanting to be in control takes over and an individual can become more assertive in demonstrating their leadership than was their intention.

Carolyn recognised that responding in kind to what her colleague was doing would do neither of them any good. But she was not going to play second fiddle and be excessively deferential. She saw it as both in her interest and her colleague's interest to demonstrate that they had worked together as a team. The practical lesson from Carolyn's experience is about recognising that in some situations people will use sharp elbows, with the right response being to respond firmly but not confrontationally.

When someone persistently uses sharp elbows, a frank, open conversation is likely to be necessary. Many people will be willing to say they will modify their approach, but whether that modification actually happens may be another story.

Someone who persistently uses sharp elbows will be doing themselves and their team no good at all. It might need a concerted response from a number of colleagues to persuade that individual to be less pushy and more generous in respecting other people's contributions.

The risks are both that other people use sharp elbows and throw us off course, and that we use sharp elbows without realising the consequences. Sometimes we can be so committed to a particular project that we fail to recognise the impact we have. If we are too assertive others can feel brushed aside. Trusting others to give clear feedback about our impact is a valuable aid to modifying our approach if we sometimes give the impression of using sharp elbows. There can also be times when we may be accused of having sharp elbows when it actually means our critic is unhappy that they are losing the argument.

Practical steps

Some practical steps to help develop your response when people take advantage of you might include:

- Anticipate when this behaviour might occur
- Be ready to be amused by pushy behaviour
- Recognise that you might be equally prone in other situations to push your own case too hard

If someone over the next week tries to take advantage of you, how might you:

- Respond to that action
- Ensure that you are not taken advantage of
- Try to give feedback and build a new, more constructive working relationship

Elbows are an important part of our anatomy. If we could not bend our elbows it would be much more difficult to retain our balance. What happens to our elbows when we are under stress is worth watching.

41

BE CAUTIOUS OF
BRIGHT LIGHTS

All that glitters is not gold

Bright lights can be a draw. The fireworks display that casts a range of colours into the sky cheers us up. The glittering lights of the Christmas season lift our spirits.

We may not enjoy being under the spotlight, but we relish the praise that might come to us because of the work we do. We may be attracted by the bright lights of fame and fortune, but might not be prepared for being put centre stage.

Often it is right that the ideas we represent are centre stage. But public scrutiny results from the combination of recognition and accountability.

❖ Roger's story:

Roger had been working on a new product. He was delighted when he was asked to give a presentation to the Operations Committee. He was excited about this opportunity and thought that he would build quickly the support of key people on this committee. He bubbled with excitement as he entered the room. The committee welcomed his energy but found his presentation chaotic and unpersuasive. Roger was convinced that all he needed to do was speak from the heart before this key group. It was a shock to him that they were sceptical and seemed unpersuaded. He recognised afterwards that much more preparation was necessary.

Being in the spotlight can have different effects on us. For some, when under the spotlight, we want to shrivel up and disappear with the consequence that we do not give of our best. For others being under the spotlight creates an energy that can become over excitable and we talk ourselves into an overly positive position with the danger of creating expectations that we cannot deliver. In both these situations the corrective is in knowing ourselves and how we respond so that when the spotlight is on us, we can predict our initial response and, to an extent, correct for it.

Bright lights might be attractive to us when we need encouragement. The glittering new solution or the confident expression of a new way forward may be attractive to us, partly because of the novelty of new ideas or the attraction of promises of success or change. We can so easily be sucked into the dreams of others when there is only partial evidence for success.

How easily are we taken in? Is it our instinctive reaction to be over trusting or over sceptical? Every new idea put to us will come with a high level of self-interest. Being sceptical about the lights others dangle before you will be helpful, up to a point.

A risk of a bright light is the resulting focus of attention on just one light. It is right that we focus on a key priority. But most jobs require that a number of priorities are met, and customers responded to. When one issue is burning brightly, the important question is about what other fires need to be kindled so that the activity is not distorted by the focus on a single high-profile area.

A risk of bright lights is that shadows are hidden. If the focus of internal scrutiny is on one area, other activities can become forgotten or ignored. Sometimes the role of a good manager is to bring a spotlight onto hidden areas so that they get their time in the limelight and feel acknowledged. Bright lights can blind us, and in the extreme can send us into the ditch. Bright lights can be very helpful in showing us the way forward, but can also throw us off course and leave us uncertain.

The risks are not only about the effect of bright lights on us, but how we can affect others by the light we bring. If we shine a focus on particular areas we will be affecting the behaviour of others. Used in a deliberate way, shining a light forward can be a powerful influence for good. But if the light we shine flashes around in a random way, we can leave people feeling discordant and uncertain.

Practical steps

Preparing to cope with bright lights might include:
- Understand how you respond to being in the limelight
- Prepare effectively so that the emotional reaction of being in the limelight does not distort the message you want to give
- Be honest about the impact you can have on others when you are in the limelight

As you reflect on a situation where you are going to be under bright lights over the next week or two, how might you:
- Prepare for that situation
- Be clear what outcomes you want from that situation
- Be ready to respond in the moment to the type of comments or hesitations that you are likely to hear

Bright lights can effect us in many different ways. Often the impact is positive in helping bring clarity and direction. But knowing when we can be blinded or thrown off course is an important part of our self-perception and understanding. Do be cheered by the bright lights while recognising that all that glitters is not gold.

42 WATCH THE AUDIT TRAIL

You have to be able to live with yourself

Watching the audit trail must be the right thing to do. We need to be clear about the reasons for our actions and be able to explain them to others. The scrutiny which we may well be put under means that we must always be able to set out the reasons for the decisions we make.

If every decision has to be utterly logical where would creativity be? If we are too fearful of the consequences of not being meticulous in setting out the audit trail, we can become stultified and completely lacking in positive drive or motivation. The big stick of fear of the auditors may be a motivator up to a point. But most of us need carrots as well as sticks to bring out the best in us. Perhaps a risk is being too driven by the need to leave an audit trail?

❖ Archie's story:

Archie had been given a product line to develop. He began with great enthusiasm but started to become apprehensive about how he was being viewed. He kept checking back with other people. He wrote down in detail the precise steps he was taking and the reasons for them. Time for thinking openly about how to develop the product was squeezed. The team began to feel they were looking back rather than forward, and were pre-occupied in giving an impression of activity rather than pushing the product development onto the next phase.

Archie began to feel more and more depressed. It was input from his boss who had spotted the problem that made all the difference. The boss' advice was for Archie to give himself space and time to develop the product without feeling he had to check back continually. The boss said that he did not need to hear again from Archie for three weeks. With this practical and emotional liberation, Archie and his team became more creative. When they reported back in three weeks, they had made some good progress.

One risk is that we are not mindful of the audit trail, but an equal risk is that we are too mindful of the audit trail. How do we reconcile this? We need to be able to give a good answer for whatever we do. Whatever action we take there does need to be a reason that we are happy to explain. When significant sums of money are involved it is essential that decisions are documented so that it is clear that financial allocations and disbursements have been made properly, consistently and transparently.

When decisions are made on projects, it is right that views of key people are considered and there is proper regard to financial resourcing, the skills available, the necessary time scales for different actions, alongside clarity about the consequences of different actions. Proper, thorough processes and regular scrutiny is a positive help rather than a hindrance.

But many decisions need to be taken in the moment when it is not possible to check the facts in great detail or to consult widely. The teacher is making instant judgements in the classroom about the approach taken to a particular topic or pupil. The doctor is making a quick judgement at surgery about what is the likely medical problem that an individual is addressing. A police officer may have to take immediate action about whether to use physical force or not.

Constant fear about whether they will be criticised for their actions would get in the way of the effective work of the teacher, the doctor or the police officer. The teacher, doctor or police officer has to be free to make decisions in real time. The audit trail for these people relates to the quality of their training and the overall effects of their actions over a period of time.

The person leading a project or building a new team needs time to prepare, to think through possibilities, to test out different options and to build a way forward before it is reasonable for them to be scrutinised. We need to create space for ourselves to be free to think in new ways and to push ideas to their next steps without the weight of scrutiny every few days.

When we have the opportunity to lead others, our audit of what they do is important, but if it is too restrictive, we can kill motivation. Liberating others has to sit alongside whatever audit trail we think is necessary.

Practical steps

Is there an activity which you are involved in at the moment where the audit trail needs to be clearer? Practical steps might include:

- Be clear about the remit and expectations
- Ensure that others endorse the same set of expectations
- Build clear agreement about how progress is to be measured

Where you think that the audit requirements are too constraining, might next steps be to:

- Redefine what are the essential outcomes and timetable
- Create space for more open thinking and dialogue
- Limit the referral points to agreed, key milestones

Sometimes we react emotionally rather than rationally to the requirement for audit which can get in the way of making progress. When we view the audit trail as a friend who can help rather than hinder us, we can sit more lightly to audit as an essential part of good management.

43

WELCOME THE HEALTH CHECK

Be open to being open

We like to think that we have set off on the right course. Scrutiny is a good thing but sometimes we think it is more appropriate for other people than ourselves. We know where we want to get to and we have a set of clear milestones and a timetable. The last thing we want is someone slowing us down and checking up on what we are doing.

Feedback is a precious gift. Sometimes we can be blinkered to the impact that we are having. We may not always realise that we are doing more harm than good, while having the best of intentions.

For us as individuals, a periodic health check can forewarn us of problems and persuade us to change some of our habits. The regular trip to the dentist may fill us with gloom, but checking up on the state of our gums can save us from much pain at a later stage.

❖ **Angela's story:**

Angela was responsible for the introduction of a new computer system. The specification had involved careful consultation with a wide range of different people. Her customers were positive about progress and there were key milestones to meet. The idea of an external health check seemed like a distraction. Reluctantly, she went along with the health check. Much of the feedback was positive which was a reassurance to both her and her customers. The health check raised three or four points of concern which she had not fully appreciated. Initially these points were a surprise but it was a relief when she had worked through them and built clarity into the next steps. Angela was pleased that the health check had happened, both because of the positive messages and for highlighting the issues that needed remedying.

We often collude with others without realising we are doing so. We persuade ourselves that we are being successful. Others want us to be successful and there is a mutual reinforcement. But it can mean moving down a pathway which is not the most appropriate. The independent view of a third party can identify when there is collusion. The prospect of a forthcoming health check can enable us to self-check whether there is a degree of collusion going on.

One of the main values of a health check is affirmation that we are doing the right things. Such reinforcement can have a powerful effect on our confidence in taking forward next steps and on our sense of shared endeavour with partners.

A health check can involve an external expert reviewing an area of work, particularly when a project is involved. But a health check can also include working with an executive coach to help you think through difficult issues. A good friend who is able to ask incisive questions can enable you to stand back and review the impact you are having.

A personal health check about your contribution at work can often be assisted by a 360° feedback exercise which many organisations now adopt. A good boss will often get feedback from a number of people about generic themes covering strengths and areas for development before writing up a performance review. This type of generic feedback will always be useful, provided you are willing to discount some of the more outlying perspectives.

Practical steps

How might you become more open to the benefits of a health check? Some practical points might be:

- Recognise when you have benefited from the scrutiny of others
- Think through what you particularly want external observations on
- Observe how others have benefited from feedback

Looking forward, it might be worth reflecting on:

- What aspect your work would benefit from a health check?
- How might you, personally, benefit from inviting feedback from your colleagues?
- Is there a coach or good friend you can work with who can help you address some of the difficult questions about the current work you are involved in?

It may be there is a pain barrier we need to go through when thinking about a health check or getting feedback. We know it is not going to be straightforward but it can be worth gritting our teeth and being open to the honest views of others, even though that prospect may not fill us with anticipation!

USE YOUR ENERGY WELL

Energy is a precious commodity. Our energy resources are neither a finite, defined amount nor are they infinite. Our energy level can go up or down depending on our own well-being and the relationship with those people around us.

Our energy is contagious. When we bring energy to solve a problem we are likely to energise those people around us. When we enter a room flat and listless, others are likely to mirror our demeanour. Perhaps we have a responsibility for the energy levels of people around us. We can so easily deflate others without realising it. Perhaps a key is how do we energise those people around us so that together, we can achieve what previously might have seemed impossible.

This section looks at trusting your internal barometer, screaming at the stars, the time for a knees-up and noticing the brick wall coming.

44 TRUST YOUR INTERNAL BAROMETER

See your intuitive reactions as valuable data

When our energy level is high nothing seems impossible. When our energy level is low we can become dejected at our inability to get things done.

Observing our energy level provides us with crucial data. We may feel flat because we are tired or exhausted, where the solution might be a good night's sleep. On other occasions we may feel flat because we are disengaged, in which case the solution might be to look at what is distracting us. Sometimes we may feel flat because the subject matter is boring where the solution is about how we find ways of making the subject more interesting. Sometimes our internal barometer is telling us an activity is a bit flat because it isn't going anywhere and it is time we changed course.

❖ Gordon's story:

Gordon was teaching a course at a university, but as Gordon gave the lectures he became more and more bored with his own words. The consequence was that the students looked uninterested and lacking in commitment. Gordon's internal barometer was telling him that all was not well with his own level of enthusiasm or the engagement of his students.

Gordon talked with a few of the students to get their perspective of what was engaging to them and their feedback helped him acknowledge that he had become tired with his own subject. He prepared for forthcoming lectures in a different way and did not just regurgitate previous notes. He brought in new angles and became more engaged himself with his own material. The lectures became livelier and he was more excited by his own words. Time went more quickly and the students left the lecture in more of a buzz.

We know when we feel energised and when our interest begins to wane and often we fight that loss of energy. We tell ourselves to try harder and concentrate. Perhaps what is needed is to change the environment or to move to a different type of activity.

When a sense of disinterest or boredom persists we may need to take stock quite radically and think about whether we should adjust our objectives and change direction in our work priorities.

Our internal barometer will measure the strength of our relationship with different individuals, and give us an initial gauge about who we trust and who we are wary of. This intuitive sense may be only partial, and may not always be right, but the data it gives us provides a starting point for deciding who we are going to trust, and in what way.

When our internal barometer is wary of somebody, might the cause be their different approach, background, or even what they are wearing? It might be that something did not go completely well in a previous episode of working together. This perception could be useful information or out-dated baggage. It can be worth reflecting on the extent to which we are willing to test our initial perception of being wary about someone, by giving them the benefit of the doubt and giving them time to prove that our wariness was misconceived.

Our internal barometer might be warning us in a particular situation that all is not what it seems. It may be saying, tread carefully, build your own understanding and do not necessarily fully accept the views of other people. The internal barometer reading might be so cold that it can be telling us that the organisation we are part of is dysfunctional and unlikely to change radically for the better of its own accord.

When your internal barometer is warm and you feel a strong sense of well-being, and have the strong support of others, do enjoy that sensation and do not take it for granted. Creating an environment where the internal barometers of those around you are positive is a precious skill. The more we can help people glow with energy, the more we can create a team spirit that will be productive.

It is perhaps paradoxical that one of the best ways of building energy in others results from how we relate to them when their energy is low. If we nurture and cherish them, we are much more likely to create a positive outcome than if we castigate them or ignore them.

Practical steps

How might you become more attuned to your internal barometer? Practical steps might include:

- Observe your own well-being part way through a week and identify what had been the causes of highs and lows
- Observe when your internal barometer drops and notice what is the effect of going into a different physical space or doing a different activity
- Observe the effect of your level of physical activity on your internal barometer

During the next week can you reflect on:

- What is likely to energise you and raise the level of your internal barometer?
- What is likely to make you flat and how can you prepare for that situation or even avoid it?
- How might you enable others to feel good about themselves so that they are energised and are in turn able to energise others?

It can sometimes be helpful to think of yourself as a barometer which is giving you different messages at different times. This element of distancing yourself from your emotions can help you view those emotions more objectively so that you are less captured by them and able to preserve your equilibrium and maintain a positive attitude. Whatever our internal barometer is saying is valuable data which we ignore at our peril.

45 POUND THE PAVEMENTS

Or even scream at the stars

However hard we try, a project we are working can go 'pear shaped': while we are in the midst of a major piece of drafting, the broadband connection goes down and we lose a chunk of work; we plan hard for a meeting which is cancelled at the last minute; we have worked hard to help a client, who then ignores what we say.

We can feel slighted, rejected, ignored, demeaned or irrelevant. Sometimes we want to crawl away into a corner. On other occasions we want to hit someone in a place where it hurts. Maybe the right solution is to pound the pavements and go for a brisk walk, or hit a tennis ball very hard, or go for a long run, or do ten lengths in the swimming pool. Perhaps a response might be to go into an empty space and scream at the stars or shout out words that we would not share with our family and friends! Sometimes we have to let out the frustration we feel and not regard it as inappropriate to do so.

❖ Teresa's story:

Teresa had worked with a group of young people who were at risk of turning delinquent. She had introduced them to some people who had been through prison who were keen to discourage others from falling into the same cycle. She tried to create the right conversations and environment to enable these young people to build a resolve not to commit crime. She had done her level best. When some of them were caught stealing, she felt very cross. Yet she knew that if she was cross with them directly it could be counter-productive. She went for a run and as she ran through a deserted field she could be heard screaming at the stars!

There are occasions when all we can do is step to one side and say, "I have done all I can." When a proposal into which we put a lot of effort has been rejected, there may be little we can do. If we boil with anger or resentment, we recognise that to express that anger at work is not going to do us much good.

Sometimes we have to let out our feelings of disappointment or rejection in a way that is overt and physical. We may want to kick the cat, but normally the cat is quicker than we are and promptly gets out of the way. We may want to kick the door, but the resulting dint in the door is likely to be with us for years to come as a painful reminder of our folly. Most of us know from an early age that letting out our frustration on those nearest to us is unlikely to be helpful, as these are the people whose support and encouragement we need more than anybody else's at these moments.

Pounding the pavements can be the best antidote. Going for a brisk walk can bring us back to our senses and help us acknowledge that circumstances outside our control led to an outcome not of our choosing. There may be one type of physical activity that helps get anger or disappointment out of our system. When we are conscious of what that physical exercise is, it is not an indulgence to do it. Keeping up the swimming, running, walking or exercise at the gym can be one of the most precious things we can do to keep our equilibrium. Tiring ourselves out physically can be the best treatment when our emotions are tangled.

We have been trained by the requirements of office behaviour or the proper disciplines of family life not to express anger, not to use curses or expletives. But sometimes in a private place verbalising what we feel can get anger and resentment out of our system and make us feel so much better. Shouting can be a cathartic act in a private space. But it need not necessarily be externalised. In our mind we can express the shouts and strong words and get them out of our system just as easily, and without unintended consequences, as if we were saying those things out loud.

So do not be inhibited from pounding the pavements or screaming at the stars when you judge it is necessary to do so but perhaps it is worth telling trusted others what you are doing and why!

Practical steps

What might you do to assess your response when your proposals are rejected or your approach seems to have failed? Might some steps be:
• Be clear what is your equivalent to pounding the pavements
• Be clear whether screaming at the stars is an approach that can work for you
• Work through how you build your equilibrium and prepare for reverses so that pounding the pavements or screaming at the stars becomes less necessary

Can you reflect on something that is happening at the moment which might not go your way and where you are likely to feel rejected? How in this situation might you:
• Prepare for this possibility
• Respond in the moment
• Return to your equilibrium as quickly as is reasonably possible

None of us are perfect human beings. However much we try to discipline our behaviour and reactions we all need escape valves that work for us and do not cause pain for others. Working out our method of pounding the pavement or screaming at the stars is necessary and not indulgent. It is part of recognising and living with the way we were made.

46 TIME FOR A KNEES-UP

A good celebration is never wasted

When did you last initiate a celebration? Sometimes life feels too busy. We have completed one task and need to move quickly onto the next. We want to leave our work behind and move into other activities in our community or with our family. And then the weekend is over and we are back at work. We can rush from one week to the next without much pause for reflection or celebration.

And yet we always remember good celebrations from the past. They mark key events for us. We remember the boss who took time to thank us and arranged a small celebration to mark a critical event. We love celebrations provided by others but can be surprisingly reluctant to initiate them ourselves.

Perhaps creating the time or opportunity for a celebration – a "knees-up" – is one of the most significant things we can do to build good will among the people we work with. It is an investment of resource and time that is rarely wasted.

❖ **Barry's story:**

Barry knew the power of celebration. Whenever a major task had been achieved there would be a good excuse for a brief get together with a few words of thanks. These were never extravagant affairs. It was often a glass of economical wine and only rarely champagne. The words he used were always simple, clear and warm with a touch of dry humour. A celebration might take four to five minutes. He judged the mood well and knew when to highlight someone's achievements and when to be very discreet in the words of praise and thanks. Barry was always on the lookout for a reason for a celebration. If three weeks passed without a celebration he knew that he needed to find good cause for the next one.

Good communication is often associated with effective celebration. The leader who brings his people together on a regular basis has a ready-made opportunity to say thank you and celebrate success.

One leader took pride in sending five handwritten notes of thanks each week. Another was always assiduous in sending email notes of thanks. A third leader prided himself on always dropping in to see three or four individuals each week to thank them for their specific contributions. The small note of thanks may be treasured for years and have a long-term effect on an individual's motivation.

Celebrations can be as much about a cup of tea or a chocolate biscuit as about a glass of wine. Extravagance could easily be criticised as waste. And yet there are moments when the jar of expensive perfume needs to be broken open and the good wine enjoyed.

Wild excess is rightly mocked, but if there is no sense of celebration, work becomes drudgery without clearly marked moments of success. The best leaders will always be prepared to invest their own money in celebrations to mark what members of their staff have achieved.

A celebration might be a brief, 10-minute event with a short speech of thanks. But there are times when a "knees-up" is appropriate. An office barn dance can be a brilliant way of bringing people of different ages and backgrounds together. A trip on the river can be a good way of mixing people up in an informal atmosphere. Going out of your comfort zone into a different place can provide a new sense of energy and build new bonds between different people. There are dangers if alcohol is available in large quantities. But the potential benefits of building stronger, informal links normally far outweigh the risks of inappropriate behaviour.

Practical steps

Some points of reflection might be:

- What type of celebration brings out the best in you?
- What form of celebration works best for your colleagues and the team you are part of?
- How might you encourage a greater sense of celebration amongst your colleagues?

Looking forward to the next week:

- What might be celebrated?
- How might you initiate some expression of thanks or the marking of a particular milestone?
- How might a celebration be an opportunity to reinforce the strength of your working relationship with different people?

It can be worth reflecting on what will give a buzz to the team you are leading or are a part of. How can a sense of joy or achievement be both encouraged and respected? Having fun at work is a perfectly legitimate aspiration. Enabling your colleagues to smile and be thankful for what they have achieved is a valuable contribution to helping them and you thrive at work.

47 NOTICE THE BRICK WALL COMING

*Bashing your head against a brick wall will
damage your head more than the wall*

Are brick walls to be climbed or avoided? They are certainly not there to be
run into as the wall will inevitably come off best.

We might have a natural tendency to think that any brick wall can be
climbed: perhaps the athletic, 15-year-old within us (buried deeply within
us!) has not lost the desire to overcome any obstacle. Perhaps experience
has taught us that brick walls are best circumvented, and yet we can have
a natural tendency to keep going in a particular direction even when it is
likely to be blocked.

How best do we treat a brick wall with respect so that we avoid bashing
our head against it? It might mean knowing how to avoid a wall, climb it
or in the extreme, dismantle it. It might mean knowing who we can work
with who's better equipped at navigating around a wall.

❖ Mohammed's story:

Mohammed was determined to make a success of the building project he
was responsible for. He wanted it to be top quality. He ensured the best
quality materials were used and that corners were not cut. The problem was
that costs were rising compared to the budget and the finance team put an
absolute limit on the expenditure. Mohammed initially wanted to ignore
this constraint but recognised that the budget was a fixed one. It was a brick
wall coming towards him.

In time, he was able to make adjustments to the planned expenditure and saved himself from a major row with the Finance Department. He had noticed, just in time, that he was in danger of running straight into a brick wall.

It is difficult to judge when an obstacle can be climbed over or circumvented and when it is an immoveable constraint. It is right to test the strength of a wall and look at the size of the drop on the other side. Sometimes obstacles are there to be removed.

But some obstacles are constraints we ignore at our peril. A brick wall that is unavoidable might be financial constraints, previous commitments, the pre-defined philosophy of the organisation, the views of the chief executive, or the known behaviours of customers. Admitting that there is a brick wall is not a sign of failure, it is an acknowledgement of realism.

It is a sign of strength to be able to say that a particular route is not possible. Sometimes it is the easy way out to say, "I am going to try harder," when creative energy is needed to think through different angles and approaches.

Brick walls are normally there for a purpose. It may be that their purpose is now out of date. But quite often a wall continues to perform a useful function, even if it is just so you don't take it for granted that the route you are set on will inevitably be the right course.

It can be humiliating to admit that there is a brick wall coming. Your pride can be hurt. It can feel brave or even foolhardy to speak against the tide. But when you perceive insurmountable problems ahead, there is a duty to forewarn even if you are subject to scepticism at the time.

Self-preservation is a necessary driver. Bashing one's head on a brick wall is in no-one's interest. We might think we are tough, but we are not necessarily that tough. Trying to do the impossible will sap our energy and leave us unable to deliver what we regard as most important. If conserving our energy for our key priorities is of particular relevance, then watching for brick walls and deciding which ones to avoid is an important part of self-preservation.

Practical steps

Ways of enhancing your awareness of forthcoming brick walls might include:

- Calibrating the significance of obstacles that you face
- Seeking the perspective of others about how significant these obstacles are
- Identifying what further information you need in order to judge the height and strength of the brick walls

If over the next week you find yourself faced with a brick wall, might it be worth asking:

- How important is the priority that this wall is blocking?
- On a scale of 1 to 10, how moveable is this brick wall?
- What are the alternative routes you can take?
- How much is pride getting in the way of reaching the right decision?

A brick wall is not to be trifled with. Deciding which to climb, which to knock down and which to circumvent is one of the pleasures of decision-making which we will not always get right.

KEEP IT IN PERSPECTIVE

Enjoying the absurd can become the basis for a new way of thinking. We can become preoccupied with the events of the moment. We are determined to do a good job. We become totally committed to what we are trying to do and don't always keep it in wider perspective. It can all become very serious and perhaps feel heavy and burdensome.

There is a risk that we can take ourselves too seriously. We are, at the end of the day, a fairly insignificant contributor to the world and even our particular bit of the world. Perhaps we can influence a number of people to good effect, but we are a small player in a large universe.

This section looks at seeing the ridiculous, being in touch with your melancholy side, allowing for joyful moments, seeing the light at the end of the tunnel and whether is it all a dream. My hope is that something in these chapters will encourage you to take your life not quite so seriously and to sit lightly to some of the emotions you are experiencing.

48 SEE THE RIDICULOUS

Truth has many angles

When we are in the heat of the moment we rarely see ourselves as others see us. We can become intense, wound up and pressured. A few days later our behaviour can seem out of proportion and a bit ridiculous. We have become so enmeshed in an issue that we do not see the different shades of grey or find our way out of a tedious piece of conflict.

When we look back, it is often the small issues that we became most uptight about. They seemed important in the moment, but with the benefit of hindsight we have found them to be but trivial issues. We say to ourselves how ridiculous we were and either get cross with ourselves or laugh at our own silliness.

❖ Gillian's story:

Gillian prided herself on running her ward in the hospital well. She had high standards about the need for efficiency. The beds needed to be laid out properly. She felt that one or two of the hospital porters were becoming a bit sloppy and were not putting the beds back in the right place. This began to annoy her and the porters got told off about not putting the beds back in just the right place. After one or two of her colleague nurses suggested that she had been too critical of the porters, Gillian recognised that she had been a bit too harsh and began to laugh at herself. Gillian began to befriend the porters who, surprise, surprise, began to take more care about putting the beds back precisely where Gillian wanted them to go.

The best leaders take big issues and crises in their stride. But they can often become preoccupied with relatively minor matters and be reluctant to let go when it comes little details. A preoccupation with certain types of detail can become a helpful displacement activity so that calmness can be kept for the most important of issues! But when we become preoccupied with points of relative detail it is all the more important to see the funny side and to laugh at yourself and your own idiosyncrasies.

When a meeting becomes too serious, one way of keeping a sense of detachment is to imagine the meeting taking place in bizarre circumstances. The meeting might be on top of a mountain or in the desert or be surrounded by elephants. Visualising the bizarre can take us into a different perspective where we can sit both inside a meeting and outside it at the same time, and thereby keep a sense of perspective.

Imagining people in ridiculous outfits can enable us to feel more at home in a context which might otherwise be daunting. Thinking of something ridiculous that you would love to do can raise your spirits when you have to cope with the most dour of discussions.

If we can help people smile in meetings we can lighten the tone and possibly make it easier to come to an agreed resolution. If we smile, others are likely to mirror our behaviour, whether they like it or not. One of the most precious gifts we can give to other people is to enable them to smile when they are coping with a sequence of demanding tasks. Most situations have a humorous dimension to them. The more we can identify that dimension, and let some laughter burst out, the more we can help a team to become more effective.

Practical steps

Some practical ways of increasing your ability to see the ridiculous might include the following:

• Imagine everyone in a room in a pantomime hat
• Imagine what would happen to your team if they were all tickled by a gigantic, many-legged spider
• Think of the most absurd thing that could happen in a meeting

If you expect a difficult meeting coming up over the next couple of weeks, what might help you bring a lighter touch to that meeting? Would it help to:

• Go into the meeting in a sense of calmness with a willingness to smile and engage in cheerful conversation with others?
• Be alert to when participants might be open to comments that could diffuse a tense atmosphere
• Allow yourself to slow down a discussion to take some of the heat out of it, with the result being a reflective and more relaxed tone

The more your frame of mind is one of enjoying a particular discussion or meeting, the more likely you are to bring a lighter ambience, and to create an atmosphere where there is a touch of humour. When you see the ridiculous, you might sometimes want to share your reaction, while signalling that you are deliberately bringing on a lighter touch.

49 BE IN TOUCH WITH YOUR MELANCHOLY SIDE

Out of the gloaming and away from the gloom

Times of melancholy are part of the emotional journey for many of us. Times of gloom can be hard to break out of. Times of gloaming can feel like an eternity. When we are in the twilight, life can feel uncertain and the next steps, unclear.

Times of melancholy can bring us back to what is most important to us. When we are sad we can feel close to those we love who are long gone, or whose state of mental health means that the degree of communication is much reduced.

❖ Helen's story:

Helen was committed to being the best possible receptionist at a doctor's surgery. She was hardworking, efficient and always purposeful and friendly. Any practical problem was there to solve. She never gave up and was determined that nobody left the surgery feeling they had been poorly served. But life for Helen was exhausting. She fought her tiredness, her energy began to dissipate and she felt she was "bumping along the bottom". There was a sadness that became unrelenting. She did not know how to break out of it. Helen recognised that over time she had to do more to conserve her energy, prioritise her work, build up interests outside her employment and find personal interests that she particularly enjoyed. Gradually, that sense of sadness and melancholy began to dissipate and her energy levels began to rise again.

The time of melancholy and sadness was a necessary part of Helen's journey. She had to slow down and be forced to address the way she used her energy before she could make the adjustments necessary for her continued well-being. She needed to let go to move forward and allow the sense of melancholy to gradually subside.

When we are in gloom we cannot just snap out of it. But we can put ourselves in situations which have helped lift our gloom before. We can talk to people whom we know can lift our spirits. We can reflect on what is becoming clearer about our use of time and energy during this period of gloom. Observing ourselves when we are in gloom can give us new insights about what matters and what is less important.

When we are in the gloaming or in twilight, we can see different reflections. We observe shadows falling in different ways. When we see through dim light we peer harder and can discern shapes and patterns which can give us new insights, and help us crystallise in our minds what our next steps should be.

Practical steps

When you are feeling melancholy and a bit flat it might it be helpful to reflect on:

- What you learned from previous periods of melancholy
- What was most important to you during these times
- How this experience might shape what is most important to you in the future

If you are hit by a period of gloom in the next couple of weeks, might it be helpful to:

- Think through how you might respond in advance to that possibility
- Acknowledge your own emotional cycle and how you best move through a period of gloom

- Allow yourself to accept that there might be some benefits from slowing down that could result from a period of relative gloom

When we are feeling melancholy or gloomy, fighting it is often not the best way forward. Acknowledging our mood and recognising honestly the limitations it places upon us, can give us a sense of proportion that enables us to live through the day's emotions knowing that we will come out on the other side.

50   ALLOW JOYFUL MOMENTS

Laugh and the world laughs with you,
cry and you cry alone

What gives you joy in your work? It might be observing someone who completes tasks they never thought possible. It might be being delighted by an individual who has become much more confident. It can flow from your own hesitancy turning into a new confidence when you speak in front of others.

Joy might be when you see a team working really well together or when a relationship that has been fractured in the past is healed and two people return to being a very effective team. Joy can flow from the excitement when a task has been completed or an unexpected agreement reached.

❖ John's story:

John was a civil engineer leading a project for the design of an oil platform. A team of people from across the world designed the various components. The rig had to fit on a very precise base. It was constructed in a meticulous way based on the many drawings. But would it fit on the foundation? Would the measurement be accurate enough to be within one centimetre? When the moment of truth came and the rig was manoeuvred into position, it fitted. John and his team were ecstatic. They had completed a very demanding assignment involving many different engineers and the end product fitted together. John's joy was based on both professional and personal satisfaction. He took immense pride in the way the team had worked together. His joy at the outcome lasted for weeks!

Joy is deep-seated. It comes from a strong sense of professional and personal engagement and fulfilment. Such joy is not superficial buzziness. It is a joy rooted in professional standards and personal values. Allowing ourselves to be joyful reinforces our sense of personal engagement with what matters to us. It reinforces our deeply held convictions and sense of direction. It helps keep up our level of engagement even when we begin to feel weary.

Finding joy in our work and in the engagement with colleagues, clients and customers, keeps us motivated and purposeful. When we see moments of joy in the workplace, they are to be treasured. They can become part of the history and tradition of the workplace. Stories retold of joyful moments in the work environment can reinforce the sense of common purpose and enable a team to build on past successes and move purposefully into new horizons.

Practical steps

Some practical ways of developing your capacity to experience joyful moments at work might include:

- See joyful moments as part of a team working effectively together and not as a distraction or an irrelevance
- Reflect on how joyful moments can be times when a team becomes stronger with good quality working relationships becoming even more effective
- Enable a sense of slowing down and reflection that can help re-energise a team for the future

As you think forward over the next few weeks:
- What might be joyful moments you can look forward to?
- What might be joyful moments that you would want to ensure are properly marked?

- How can you enable others to see joy in events where they would be tempted to rush on to the next activity and not enjoy the moment?

Joy comes from being comfortable in your own skin and being glad to be doing what you are doing. It is about acknowledging that you are in a place where you can make a difference for good and enjoying the opportunities that your work brings to encourage and enable others.

51

SEE THE LIGHT AT THE END OF THE TUNNEL

Watch the light as it shines more brightly

You are working on a demanding project. A new product is to be launched and you have had a central role engaging different parties and ensuring that all the contributors are working towards a common end. The work is relentless. You can't see it coming to an end, but you know you have a tight deadline.

When we are focused on day-to-day progress we often cannot see very far ahead. The risk is we lose that sense of long-term direction and outcome. We need to recognise that there is light at the end of the tunnel, in order to keep up our resolve to reach the destination we have set for ourselves. Light at the end of the tunnel is not just about a factual destination: it is about the sense of liberation and energy that will flow when we have done what we set out to do.

❖ Richard's story:

Richard knew that he could get bogged down in day-to-day tasks if he was not careful. He was conscious that the clearer his mental picture of the outcome he was working towards, the more energised he would be during the whole process. When Richard visualised the building he was designing, it helped to give him the energy to spend the time designing each individual component. Light at the end of the tunnel for Richard was about seeing the building finished, gleaming in the sunlight. He knew from previous experience that his designs worked. He knew that he had to keep his head down and focus on getting each component part right. He knew what he would feel when the task was complete which helped him renew his energy as the demanding design work was completed one piece after another.

Tunnels get us from 'A' to 'B' efficiently. Sometimes we need to create tunnels in our mind so we are not distracted. A good tunnel has strong walls and a roof that is not going to cave in. Tunnel vision may be essential to our survival as we work towards a particular outcome.

But we have a choice about when we go through a tunnel or when we climb over the mountains. We are making choices all the time about what we do and think, and how we view the reality around us.

Seeing the light at the end of the tunnel is about never giving up. It is recognising the determination within us, the opportunities around us and our own need to make a difference. It is recognising "what lights our fire" and keeping up that sense of purpose and resolve that is consistent with our values and aspirations.

Practical steps

Some practical ways of enhancing your ability to see light at the end of the tunnel might be:

- Accept your own pattern from previous experiences, acknowledging what helps you see light at the end of the tunnel
- Keep coming back to what is most important for you on this journey
- Have a clear picture in your mind as to the outcomes that are most important for you

As you seek out the light at the end of the tunnel, might you reflect on:

- Are you and your colleagues aiming to reach the same destination?
- How might you describe the end result so that it best encourages and energises others?

- How might you build a stronger sense of shared vision about the outcomes which need to be delivered?

Sometimes the light in the distance is tiny or faint. But when the light becomes gradually brighter we know we are going in the right direction. Sometimes it is a matter of keeping at it, going a step at a time so the light gradually fills the space and we know we are making progress.

52 IS IT ALL A DREAM?

What is the reality?

To survive we need to be able to come in and out of current reality. We need to be able to dream dreams and see beyond our current circumstances, but we also need to be rooted in reality. Maintaining our sanity depends on understanding the context within which we live so we recognise the hard, commercial reality in which we work. At the same time, to keep our sanity, we need to be able to see beyond the immediate and sense what is possible in the future.

Success comes from being honest about problems, resolute about the way forward, and engaged with those around us, combined with a hopefulness about the future that is more than just wishful thinking. We can get far with dogged, hard work. But we need to be inspired by the prospect of what can be changed if we are to maintain our energy over a long period.

We have to be able to dream dreams about what might be achievable through the contribution we can make. We need to be enriched by the prospect that the child we teach will grow into a responsible adult, or that the patient will get better, or the product will become more effective, or the service will be more appreciated by customers, or that individuals will grow in confidence because of the way we have been able to encourage or mentor them.

Thriving depends on dreaming dreams that are rooted in reality and in our values. If we believe that individuals can change, that broken working relationships can be mended, that dysfunctional organisations can be healed, that arrogant people can learn humility and that out of failure there can be new beginnings, then our dreams have the potential of coming true.

Dreams are not about wishful thinking. They include thinking beyond our current expectations or frame of reference. They are about being bold and courageous to try to create more purposeful, creative and supportive communities in both the workplace and beyond.

We can dismiss our hopes and aspirations as just dreams. But perhaps those hopes and aspirations can provide us with a new reality. When we are rooted in our values, we can have a clear vision about what we want to contribute, know when we can bring a value-added contribution and appreciate our own sources of vitality. Then we can make a difference in our chosen sphere and can thrive in our work.

Thriving is not about linear progression. There will be moments when our efforts seem irrelevant, our contribution is ignored and the future looks bleak. We then may need to look at issues from different angles and see those moments as part of a longer journey which will have its ups and downs. Growing the resilience to thrive in tough times is not straightforward. Sometimes it is about "gritting our teeth". On other occasions it is letting the joy burst out of us.

Reality is what we experience at work, but is also what is going on in our head. Whatever is happening in the work environment, our mind may be dominated by noise or frustration or aggravation, or be uplifted by a sense of progress and mutual support.

Thriving is about living with both realities: the reality in the workplace and the reality of what we are experiencing in our hearts and minds, and then keeping them in reasonable balance.

I hope that this book has provided you with a set of reflections and prompts to enable you to dream dreams, understand your own reality, and hold your different aspirations and reactions in reasonable equilibrium.

Practical steps

Now that you have read the book, questions you might reflect on might be:

- What dreams do I have about how I might thrive in my work in the future?
- How will I ensure that I both understand my current reality and can dream dreams beyond that reality?
- What are the values, hopes and aspirations that will keep me looking beyond the immediate?
- How will I best maintain my equilibrium as I keep one foot in the present and one in the future?

I trust that the reflections will be a source of both stimulus and amusement and will lead you to think in new ways. They are not meant to be taken too seriously. If they leave you with a couple of practical ideas, that is fine.

LIBRARY, UNIVERSITY OF CHESTER

ACKNOWLEDGMENTS

The book benefits hugely from conversations with leaders in a range of sectors and countries. I am indebted to all those with whom I have been able to discuss themes in the book.

I am grateful to Sylvo Thijsen, the Chief Executive of Grontmij, an international design and engineering consultancy company, who has helped stimulate my thinking on how best to thrive at work and written the foreword to the book.

Jackie Tookey and Helen Burtenshaw have provided superb practical help in getting to a final manuscript and always been positive about this book.

My colleagues at Praesta Partners who have been a constant source of encouragement and common sense. Martin Liu has been an excellent editor to work with.

Frances, my wife, has shown immense patience as the book was put together. This included making the final amendments at the end of days after walking along the coastline of the Shetland Islands.

OTHER BOOKS BY PETER SHAW

Mirroring Jesus as Leader, Cambridge, Grove, 2004

Conversation Matters: How to Engage Effectively with One Another, London, Continuum, 2005

The Four Vs of Leadership: Vision, Values, Value-added, Vitality, Chichester, Capstone, 2006

Finding Your Future: The Second Time Around, London, Darton, Longman and Todd, 2006

Business Coaching: Achieving Practical Results Through Effective Engagement, Chichester, Capstone, 2007 (Co-authored with Robin Linnecar)

Making Difficult Decisions: How to be Decisive and get the Business Done, Chichester, Capstone, 2008

Riding the Rapids: How to Navigate Through Turbulent Times, London, Praesta, 2008 (Co-authored with Jane Stephens)

Deciding Well: A Christian Perspective on Making Decisions as a Leader, Vancouver, Regent College Publishing, 2009

Raise Your Game: How to Succeed at Work, Chichester, Capstone, 2009

Seizing the Future, London, Praesta 2010 (Co-authored with Robin Hindle-Fisher)

Effective Christian Leadership in the Global Marketplace, Authentic/ Paternoster, 2010

Defining Moments: Navigating Through Business and Organisational Life, Basingstoke, Palgrave/Macmillan, 2010

Living Leadership: Finding Equilibrium, London, Praesta, 2011

The Reflective Leader: Standing Back to Move Forward, Norwich, Canterbury Press, 2011 (Co-authored with Alan Smith)

FORTHCOMING BOOKS

Getting the Balance Right, London, Marshall Cavendish, 2012

Leading Well in Demanding Times, Cambridge, Grove, 2013

Effective Leadership Teams: A Christian Perspective, London, Darton, Longman and Todd, 2013

ABOUT THE AUTHOR

Peter Shaw works with individuals, teams and groups to help them grow their strengths and tackle demanding issues confidently. His work on how leaders step up successfully into demanding leadership roles and sustain that success has recently been recognised with a Doctorate by Publication from Chester University.

Peter's clients enjoy frank, challenging conversations leading to fresh thinking and new insights. It is the dynamic nature of the conversations that provide a stimulus for creative reflection and new action. He often works with Chief Executives and Board members taking on new roles and leading major organisational change.

Peter has worked with Chief Executives and senior leaders in a range of different sectors and countries. He has led workshops on such themes as "Riding the Rapids", "Seizing the Future", "Thriving in your Work" and, "Building Resilience" across five continents.

Peter has held a wide range of Board posts covering finance, personnel, policy, communications and delivery. He worked in five UK Government departments (Treasury, Education, Employment, Environment and Transport). He delivered major national changes such as radically different pay arrangements for teachers, a huge expansion in nursery education and employment initiatives which helped bring unemployment below a million.

He led the work on the merger of the UK Government Departments of Education and Employment. As Finance Director he managed a £40 billion budget and introduced radical changes in funding and accountability arrangements. In three Director General posts he led strategic development and implementation in major policy areas.

Peter has written a sequence of influential leadership books. He is a Visiting Professor of Leadership Development at Newcastle University Business School and has worked with senior staff at Brighton University and postgraduate students at Warwick University Business School and at Regent College in Vancouver. He was awarded a CB by the Queen in 2000 for his contribution to public service.

Peter is a Reader (licensed lay minister) in the Anglian church and has worked with senior church leaders in the UK and North America. His inspiration comes from long distance walks: he has completed ten long-distance walks in the UK including the St Cuthbert's Way, the South Downs Way and the Great Glen Way.